Good Housekeeping

The Best of the
1940s

First published in the United Kingdom in 2007 by
Collins & Brown
10 Southcombe Street
London W14 0RA

An imprint of Anova Books Company Ltd

The Good Housekeeping website address is
www.goodhousekeeping.co.uk

Commissioning Editor Miriam Hyslop
Design Manager Gemma Wilson
Designer Jeremy Tilston
Senior Production Controller Morna McPherson

ISBN 978-1-84340-458-3

A CIP catalogue for this book is available from
the British Library.

10 9 8 7 6 5 4 3 2 1

Reproduction by Rival Colour, London
Printed and bound by Qualibris, France

This book can be ordered direct from the publisher.
Contact the marketing department, but try your
bookshop first.

www.anovabooks.com

Good Housekeeping

The Best of the
1940s

COLLINS & BROWN

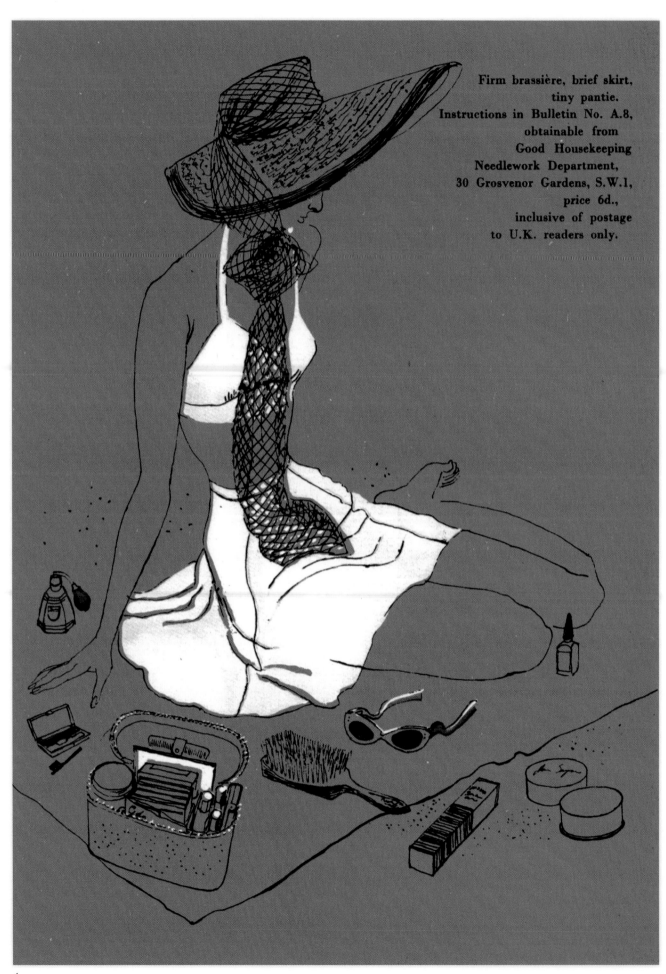

Firm brassière, brief skirt,
tiny pantie.
Instructions in Bulletin No. A.8,
obtainable from
Good Housekeeping
Needlework Department,
30 Grosvenor Gardens, S.W.1,
price 6d.,
inclusive of postage
to U.K. readers only.

Introduction

In 1939, at the start of World War II, the staff of *Good Housekeeping* left London and set up their office in St Donat's Castle in Wales, a property owned by the magazine's proprietor, William Randolph Hearst. From there, patriotic slogans, energy-saving ideas and nutritious recipes were created to help the nation at war.

The wartime paper rationing resulted in a reduction in the magazine's size but it was allowed to continue publishing throughout the war years due, in part, to the Good Housekeeping Institute's collaboration with the Ministry of Food, showing the nation how to make delicious and nutritious meals with their rations.

Wartime *Good Housekeeping* addressed the concerns of its readers with families separated by active service and evacuation, and with women adapting to their new roles in civil defence, the forces, in factories or on the land. But the magazine was not solely about cooking and nutrition. As always it produced plenty of escapism in the form of short stories and light-hearted articles as well as more serious features on issues such as infertility, adoption and female bosses. Fashion advice focused on making do rather than new styles and most of the advice on saving energy is still relevant sixty years later, in today's eco-friendly climate.

The Best of the 1940s is a fascinating collection of articles and advertisements that convey the spirit of the decade, from the cheerful determination to survive the war to the optimism of the years after it was over.

Louise

LOUISE CHUNN

WOMEN

The Duchess of Marlborough is Chief Commandant of the A.T.S.

and the

ENGLISH women have a tremendous task before them! They have to safeguard their rights and liberties during the period of transition through which we are passing. Because—let us face it: we are witnessing the birth of a new world. A new world, the foundations of which were laid not by us, but by Lenin, Stalin, Mussolini and Hitler. It is in the interest of all women, whether housewives or wage-earners, to stand guard over the advantages they have secured during the last hundred years.

The average woman is no feminist. The average woman longs for a home, a husband, children and sufficient cash to make life fairly comfortable. She may think this " chatter about rights and opportunities " does not affect her. Yet it does, for two reasons. In the first place, she may have a daughter, a niece, an aunt, a cousin or some other dependent, who wants to have a career and earn her living in competition with men. She may have to keep the said daughter, niece, etc., if she cannot enter some profession or business. So she must think of openings in terms of her relatives and her pocket. In the second place, she must remember that loss of rights for women in public life very soon reacts on them in private life, on their capacity as wives and mothers. Look at the dictator-countries, how little control mothers have over the education of their children! They are whisked away to school, to youth movements, to summer camps, to Labour Service,

and the mamas cannot utter a word of criticism. An Austrian friend of mine has a lovely daughter of sixteen. The child made a habit of staying in her day-school until midnight. When her mother enquired what she was doing, her reply was: " I can tell you nothing. I am pledged to secrecy." At last my friend interrogated the headmistress, who retorted: " If you dare once more to snoop after your daughter, who is a decent Hitler girl, I shall have you sent to a concentration camp."

The World War brought within women's reach all the openings the suffragettes had struggled for. While men were fighting on the front, women carried on in their places at home, thus disproving the arguments by which anti-feminists had countered their demands. Of course, as soon as peace came, they had to give up most of these positions. Yet, as a result of their

efforts, they were granted full political equality, and the right to work side by side with men. Looking back on it now, it seems remarkable how much of their war-gains English women retained.

Then things began to happen on the Continent. The brightest side of the Bolshevik Revolution was Lenin's attitude to women. He declared that he wanted to enable any charwoman to become president of the Soviet Republic! Overnight Russian women were given the chance of educating themselves, of entering professions, of holding positions, of working in trade, everywhere on terms of complete equality with men. In time, as the Bolsheviks began to long for respectability, measures were taken to strengthen the family, and to increase the population. Also, Russian men were tiring of the way their women—the *babas*—lived at clubs and political

meetings! Once premiums were offered for more than five children, it became well-nigh impossible for mothers to work outside their homes. Little by little the average Russian woman had to give up the idea of having a career besides looking after her children. But a few Russian women have retained important positions. Most outstanding among these is Madame Molotov, who was the head of the vast Cosmetics Trust, and was then responsible for the Ministry of Fish Supplies. In the eyes of the law, both in the political and the economic field, Russian women have equal rights with men.

Italian Fascism frankly set out to limit women's scope to family life. "Bear children for the nation!" was the slogan of the Black Shirts. To ensure the increase of the population, primarily needed to provide more soldiers for the armed forces, subsidies were paid to families for every additional child; taxes were levied in accordance with the number of offspring; bachelors and spinsters were made to pay "special contributions," etc. No device was left untried to raise the number of little Italians in this world. The reason why, originally, public opinion in the democracies paid little heed to Mussolini's "family policy," was that Italian women had never taken a great interest in public life or economic openings. Therefore few of them were displaced in the professions and in business; women factory workers were retained, care being taken of their babies during working hours. From political life the Fascists excluded women in so many words; nor were they allowed to have organisations of their own.

Economic necessity gradually broke down this attitude. A few years ago the *Fascio Feminile* (Women's Corporation) was set up, and any housewife could join it. What the Fascists thought they would do I know not; I am only aware that Italian officials watch with annoyance how women make their weight felt! Recently Italian countrywomen—*Le Massaie*—were also organised; which organisation has proved very effective.

Italian women are coming to the fore. Because so many men are enrolled in the army, they are stepping into their (*Continued on page* **114**)

THE COUNTESS OF LISTOWEL
discusses the position of women in England, Russia, Italy and Germany since the Great War

Brave New World

Countess Edda Ciano, Mussolini's daughter, is perhaps the most influential woman in present-day Italy

Frau Scholtz-Klink was chosen as the ideal representative of German womanhood according to Nazi ideas

Mme Molotov (Paulina Zhemchugina) was first head of the Cosmetics Trust, then Director of Fish Supplies

I'd like to know

I should be grateful to know the best way of removing ink stains from a fawn rug. The stains occurred a month ago and were rubbed with a duster.

Also, what would you advise for a brick path which is slippery through a mossy growth?

The ink stains should be treated alternately with a solution of potassium permanganate—½ teaspoonful to 1 pint water—and hydrogen peroxide diluted four or five times with water. Apply the permanganate solution to the marks with a fountain-pen filler. Remove excess in a second or two with a damp cloth, and apply the hydrogen peroxide solution to remove the brown stain produced by the permanganate. Rinse with water and repeat the process several times, if necessary, finally rinsing the rug thoroughly free from the chemicals. Patience may be needed, as the stain is old, but do not leave the chemicals on for more than a few seconds at a time.

For the path apply a solution of sodium chlorate, a very efficient weed killer obtainable from most chemists.

There are light oak block floors in our shop, opened six months ago, which seem to show every mark. What is the best way of dealing with them?

My cleaner also finds it difficult to remove rings left by lotion bottles on the natural wood show cases.

When a wood floor is particularly soiled it should be rubbed the way of the grain with medium-grade steel wool dipped in turpentine or white spirit before it is repolished. This treatment should only be applied very occasionally, but the floors need to be regularly polished with a white wax preparation. This helps to retain their light colour, provided clean cloths are used and the floors are swept and dusted before the wax is used.

Presumably the rings on your show cases only occur where opened bottles are stored, and are caused by drops of spilt liquid. Many toilet preparations have a basis of spirit, and are likely to remove stain and polish. Medium steel wool, as suggested for the floor, would remove the marks, and as a protective measure the wood should be polished regularly or covered with glass.

Can you tell me the best way to clean a brick fireplace? My maid has scrubbed it with soap and water, and the bricks now have a smeary white appearance.

Soap and soap powders should never be used for a brick fireplace, for, since bricks are absorbent, thorough rinsing is almost an impossibility, and, as you have discovered, they acquire a white deposit if cleaned in this way.

To remedy this, or to clean a fireplace discoloured by soot, rub the bricks with a cloth dipped in a solution of hydrochloric acid, or spirits of salt, containing 1 part acid to 5 or 6 of water. This acid is extremely poisonous and corrosive, and should only be entrusted to a responsible person, and all trace of it should be rinsed away after use. Precautions must also be taken not to allow it to remain in contact with the cement between the bricks, as it will tend to dissolve it and may loosen them.

Can you tell me how to treat a dressing-table slightly marked by a very weak solution of carbolic disinfectant?

This type of disinfectant is highly alkaline in reaction and would tend to remove polish, etc., from furniture. If the marks are only small you may be able to remedy them by treating in the same way as for heat marks on a polished table. A drop or two (not more) of methylated spirit should be placed on a pad of soft material or cotton-wool. This should be covered by a layer of muslin and the pad so prepared rubbed well over and around the table.

As this method of treatment depends for its effect on removing polish and stain from the undamaged part of the wood to the damaged, it is not likely to be successful if the marks are extensive. In this case rubbing down the whole surface and repolishing would be necessary, and this work is better entrusted to a firm of polishers.

The bath in our rented house has been sadly neglected, and there is a brownish mark at water level, and stains under each tap. What remedy do you suggest?

The brown marks are probably rust caused by iron in the water, and should be easily removed by treating with a hot, strong solution of oxalic acid. Being poisonous, this acid must be used very carefully and rinsed away thoroughly.

If the stains under the taps are caused by the hardness of the water, they can be removed with a weak acid, such as vinegar. If the marks prove very resistant, as is likely if they have been left for some time, use a stronger acid, such as spirits of salt diluted seven or eight times with water. I do not, however, suggest using this if it can be avoided, as there is a possibility of damage to the porcelain. If used, a drop or so only should be applied immediately over each stain, taking care that the acid does not come in contact with the porcelain and rinsing away very quickly and thoroughly afterwards.

Two years ago I laid cork carpet in my hall. This has, however, proved most unpractical, as it shows every mark and never looks clean. Can you advise me as to the best way of treating it?

Cork carpet is one of the most difficult of all floor coverings to keep in good condition. Scrubbing only opens the pores, with the result that it becomes more and more absorbent, and dirt and dust penetrate. Linseed oil is sometimes used to fill up the pores which give cork carpet more or less the characteristics of linoleum. This treatment is rather laborious, as it is necessary to give two or three applications of the oil, allowing an interval of a week or so between them for the oil to oxidise. Finally, after a further interval, wax polish should be applied, and once a good surface has been obtained wax polish, made into a semi-liquid consistency by dilution with turpentine or white spirit, should be rubbed in once a week and the cork well polished twenty or thirty minutes later.

I have unfortunately spilt some lime juice on a dark marble-topped table. Could you tell me how to remove these and other marks?

The acidity of the lime juice has no doubt had a slight solvent action on the marble, but you may find that you are able to mask the marks to some extent by rubbing over with a cloth dipped in a little olive oil.

If this is not effective or if there are a number of resistant stains or marks, the whole surface of the table should be treated with a weak acid, such as vinegar. If this is used it should only be allowed to remain in contact with the marble for a few seconds, and it should be quickly rinsed away with fresh water.

Treatment with vinegar or lemon juice in this way can be applied to a marble mantelpiece, washstand, or other discoloured marble surface. The efficacy of the treatment depending on surface solvent action on the marble, however, quick rinsing afterwards is always imperative.

After using acid the appearance of the marble will be improved by rubbing well with a little oil and polishing with a soft cloth.

How can I clean limed oak furniture? So far I have only dusted it, but the table top, chair legs, etc., are soiled and finger-marked.

My pale green and off-white carpets are spotted and slightly marked, and I should like your advice.

If the furniture is badly soiled it may be necessary to rub it down carefully with very fine sandpaper, but if only slightly soiled rub over with a cloth dipped in petrol or turpentine substitute. Use petrol with the greatest care, as it is highly inflammable. After treating in this way polishing would help to protect the wood, although it might alter the character of the surface slightly.

For marks on the carpet, use a reliable make of carpet soap or liquid cleanser. When removing spots, it is often necessary to go over the whole carpet, as otherwise the result is very patchy. An area about two feet square should be dealt with at a time, and each patch should overlap the next.

Here are useful hints on cleaning problems dealt with in "question and answer" form

by P. L. GARBUTT, A.I.C.

First Class Diploma King's College of Household and Social Science; late staff Battersea Polytechnic

IT would not be meet in wartime to recommend either costly or elaborate meals, but every housewife is justified in keeping up the Easter tradition of serving something a little better than usual for the first feast of the year. Let us concentrate, therefore, on foods which are not rationed, for they are the most practical when guests are invited. This cuts out butcher's meat from the menu, but poultry can replace it, and eggs are both cheap and plentiful, whilst supplies of milk, cream, fish, some cuts of bacon, vegetables and cereals are unrestricted. So there should be little difficulty in the making of the menu for Easter entertaining. Whilst the meals described in this article are a little out of the ordinary, they have been selected with due regard to economy and ease of cooking.

Stewed figs have been chosen for breakfast because they require very little sugar for sweetening. One tablespoonful to ¼ pint of water makes sufficient syrup to stew ½ lb. of figs, if they have been well soaked. If not, add more water, as the figs will absorb it. The soaking of dried fruit, figs or prunes is not essential, for we have proved that if cooked very slowly without soaking they are just as good. If it is your custom to soak dried fruit several hours before cooking you may prefer to continue doing so, but wash it first and use the soaking water for cooking, for

it will contain some of the natural sugar of the fruit. Add a tablespoonful of sugar to the soaking water and simmer over a low heat until the figs are tender. Serve with cream or evaporated milk.

Eggs en Petites Cocottes are a change from boiled or fried eggs. The only criticism that can be offered is that the oven has to be heated, but as

they take very little time to cook this small extravagance could be overlooked for a special occasion.

4 or 5 eggs	A little cream or evaporated milk
Pepper and salt	
	Chopped parsley

Grease the cocottes, and put a small teaspoonful of cream (taken from the top of the milk) or evaporated

Spatchcock of Chicken is a little unusual and very popular when served with Duchess Potatoes and Tomato or Espagnole Sauce

Left: For breakfast Steamed Figs and Eggs en Cocotte would be a wise choice, where are good supplies of both foods, and sugar is not needed for steamed figs

milk in the bottom of each. Sprinkle the cream with a little pepper and salt. Remove the eggs from the shells and put one inside each cocotte. Add a little more pepper and salt, and top with more cream. Put the cocottes into a meat tin containing sufficient water to come half-way up the sides and place the tin in a quick oven for about five to six minutes, or until the eggs are lightly set. Sprinkle the top of each cocotte with a little finely chopped parsley before sending to table.

Cod Cakes are made in the same way as other fish cakes, and the cod can be fresh, tinned or salted, or, if preferred, tinned lobster, crab, or salmon can replace it. Allow 2 to 2½ oz. flaked fish, 2 tablespoonfuls mashed potatoes and ½ tablespoonful breadcrumbs per person. Put these ingredients into a basin with pepper, salt, pinch of mace and chopped parsley, and sufficient beaten egg to bind the mixture stiffly. Turn it on to a plate, divide it into a number of equal pieces, depending on the amount of mixture. When cold shape into flat cakes, brush over with beaten egg, coat with breadcrumbs and fry in deep fat until golden-brown. Drain on

Breakfast

Stewed Figs with Cream
Cereal or Porridge
Eggs en Petites
Cocottes or Cod Cakes
Toast and Marmalade

Dinner

Beetroot Soup
Fried Sweetbreads with Spinach
Spatchcock of Chicken or Plain Roast Chicken
French Salad
Duchess Potatoes and Creamed Carrots
Cold Caramel Custard or Orange Soufflé

Supper

Lobster Bouchées
Cold Boiled Gammon
Casserole of Vegetables

kitchen-paper. Serve on paper d'oyleys and garnish with parsley.

Beetroot Soup. For this you need: 1 oz. flour, 1 onion or shallot, ¼ pint evaporated milk, 2 beetroots of medium size, 1 oz. margarine, 2 pints stock, 1 to 2 tablespoonfuls vinegar, Pepper, salt and a little made mustard.

Melt the margarine and fry the finely chopped onion or shallot very pale golden-brown. Stir in the flour, add the cold stock, bring to the boil, stirring meanwhile to prevent lumps from forming, and simmer for fifteen minutes. Peel and slice the beetroot, put it into a basin and cover with the vinegar, pepper and salt. When the stock and onion have been cooking for about quarter of an hour add the soaked beetroot and vinegar. Continue cooking for another twenty minutes. Rub through a sieve, add the evaporated milk, re-heat and serve in a hot tureen. Sprinkle the top with chopped parsley.

Fried Sweetbreads with Spinach. This makes an attractive entrée, but it can be dispensed with without spoiling the dinner in the least degree. Scald two sweetbreads, put into cold water, bring to the boil. Simmer for

Here is a luxurious-looking menu that practically eliminates rationed foods

A Good Suit will see you through

Soft fullness through the body, a neat waist and hip-line. A perfect suit of the real tailored type (far left). Cut from a beautiful grey angora tweed in a fine, neat design. A huge cluster of scarlet suède poppies match the attractive crêpe gilet front. Matita model from Harrods

You'll be a tonic for sore eyes if you choose the lipstick-red frieze suit with its slick waisted jacket and new narrow skirt. The black and white check surah shirt blouse makes a " just right " finish. Dorville model from Harrods

IF with you, as with so many of us this year, it's a case of "just one new outfit," you will probably not do better than to concentrate on a suit. Of all clothes, a good suit dates least, can be worn on the most varied occasions, and lends itself particularly readily to all kinds of quick changes."

This season, since the suit will prove as popular, designers have lavished even more skill and ingenuity than usual on their models, with the result that there is a wonderfully rich choice and no lack of those exciting little touches that make new clothes a real " thrill."

Most Paris houses, and some of the English ones, too, favour the rather strictly tailored jacket, cut somewhat longer than the average, to come well down over the hip bone. Fastenings are generally, although not invariably, high; shoulders remain nice and square without any exaggeration; and by means of shaping, darting, or just cutting skill, waists contrive to look slender and feminine.

So far as skirts are concerned, the ultra-full ones of a season ago have mostly faded from the picture. It is now a choice of a business-like or easy-to-wear circular cut, or our old favourite the slim skirt, with walking room allowed by low-placed pleats.

I said that most houses still favour the longer jacket, but the brief " top " finds a bigger place in the fashion picture than for quite a long while. Victor Stiebel, for instance, is an exponent of the youthful-looking short jacket, and gets the most attractive effects with his bright-coloured, (Continued on page **101**)

Specially made for the more mature figure. A braid-bound tailleur in a soft bird's-eye design, " pepper and salt " angora tweed. The waistcoat blouse in lovely rosy silk ottoman " dresses up " the suit for the smartest occasion. Matita model from Harrods

Gay as a huntsman's pink coat, this gilt-buttoned, poppy-red jacket, worn with an original side-pleated, grey flannel skirt. Both skirt and jacket can be teamed up with other clothes. A Dorville model from Marshall & Snelgrove Ltd.

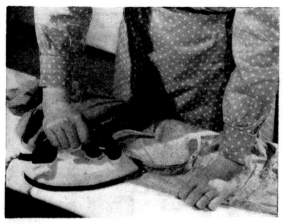

1 Before ironing, see that shirt is of uniform dampness. Press seams, hems, yoke and front pleat on the wrong side. Turn garment right side out. Iron neck band on the wrong and then on the right side, stretching it well. Now fold yoke along the lower seam and place flat on ironing surface as shown above, and continue pressing it until thoroughly dry

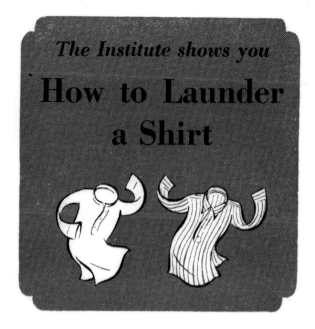

IN the average man's estimation a laundry stands or falls according to the finish achieved with his shirts. So, too, with the home laundress! Don't let this dismay you, however, for if you are prepared to work carefully there is no reason why you should not turn out a beautifully laundered garment of which you can be justly proud.

Practise on an old shirt first, or, if you have a schoolboy son, try out your skill on his, for he will possibly not be quite so critical as his father.

The fabrics used for shirtings are almost as varied as those for your own garments. Each requires slightly different laundry treatment, so consult the tabulated directions opposite. Then look carefully at the illustrations and underlying captions, which clearly show you just how to iron and finish correctly.

If you undertake a really heavy wash at home, you may possibly possess an open-ended ironer. By using this you can save time, after you have had a little practice. More important still, perhaps, if you are tired after a morning's work, you can sit down at your job. You will, however, find it important to place the shirt carefully if you are to achieve a good finish.

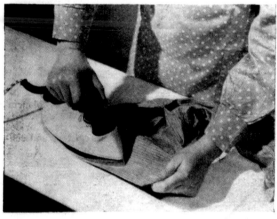

2 Iron cuffs lightly on wrong side and then heavily on right. Fold sleeve lengthwise along underarm seam and iron to within half-inch of fold only, to avoid making crease down centre. Turn sleeve over and iron the other side, pressing toe of iron well into cuff gathering. Now refold sleeve so that the unironed strip comes in the centre and iron this part

3 You are now ready to iron the body of the shirt. Place over a skirt board and iron the back first. After ironing the front, arrange the pleat carefully, pulling it taut before pressing into position. If the sleeves crease slightly while you are ironing the body, you can easily remedy this when doing the " touching up," as described in the next caption

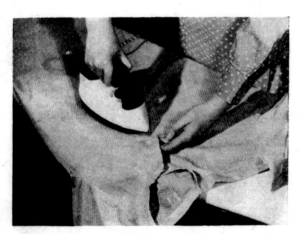

4 The last stage of ironing or touching up is extremely important, and should never be omitted if you aim at a professional finish. Lay the shirt on the ironing table or board and with a warm iron press out folds and creases that may have been made inadvertently. Pay particular attention to the front of the shirt, the yoke, the cuffs and the collar

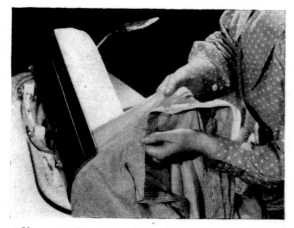

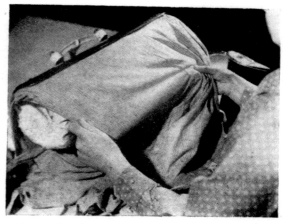

5 If you are using a rotary ironer, begin with the collar band. Place this over the open end of the ironer, stretch taut and press thoroughly. Next iron the yoke, folding this as described for the corresponding process of hand-ironing. Place it over the open end of ironer as shown in illustration. You need to keep a slight tension on the yoke while ironing

6 Press body of shirt, beginning with the back as shown above. Iron from the tail up towards the armpit. Make a central fold down front of shirt and iron upper part over open end of ironer. Deal with back in the same way. Fold the sleeves so that the seam is situated centrally and pass them once or twice through the rollers, until they are dry

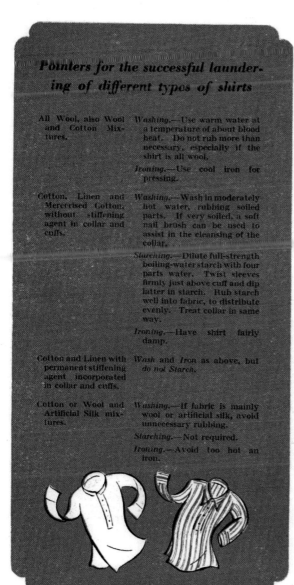

Pointers for the successful laundering of different types of shirts

All Wool, also Wool and Cotton Mixtures.	*Washing.*—Use warm water at a temperature of about blood heat. Do not rub more than necessary, especially if the shirt is all wool.
	Ironing.—Use cool iron for pressing.
Cotton, Linen and Mercerised Cotton, without stiffening agent in collar and cuffs.	*Washing.*—Wash in moderately hot water, rubbing soiled parts. If very soiled, a soft nail brush can be used to assist in the cleansing of the collar.
	Starching.—Dilute full-strength boiling-water starch with four parts water. Twist sleeves firmly just above cuff and dip latter in starch. Rub starch well into fabric, to distribute evenly. Treat collar in same way.
	Ironing.—Have shirt fairly damp.
Cotton and Linen with permanent stiffening agent incorporated in collar and cuffs.	*Wash* and *Iron* as above, but do not *Starch*.
Cotton or Wool and Artificial Silk mixtures.	*Washing.*—If fabric is mainly wool or artificial silk, avoid unnecessary rubbing.
	Starching.—Not required.
	Ironing.—Avoid too hot an iron.

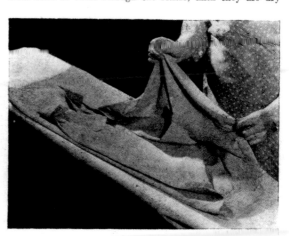

7 After touching up, you are now ready to fold the shirt. First button it, then place front side downwards on ironing table. Turn in the side seams towards the centre back, taking about one-fourth of the total width of shirt in each fold, and then lay the sleeve lengthwise along the shirt, making a right-angled turn at top of armhole, as illustrated above

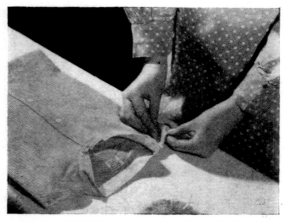

8 Turn up tail of shirt over the cuffs and then double over to form a neat rectangular shape, as shown in the illustration. Pin corners before putting away to prevent the shirt from becoming unfolded and creased. If you have followed these instructions carefully, you should have no difficulty in obtaining a perfectly ironed shirt after you have had a little practice

Shopping for Two
in Summertime

ARE first experiments in catering for two leaving *you* perplexed over the intricacies of planning menus and marketing? If so, you are at one with the many young wives who have been writing to us recently for help and advice, and here are plans and charts which will help you face your problems.

With regard to marketing, while naturally you want to provide plenty, you must cut out waste and extravagance. We are therefore giving you a chart of some of the staple foods, together with the quantities to buy for two people with average appetites. Generally speaking, you should aim at serving certain basic foods at least once a day: a pint of milk *each*, used in beverages, milky puddings, soups, and with cereals for breakfast; a raw vegetable or a green salad; a meat, fish or cheese dish; a serving of starchy vegetable (or you may include macaroni, etc.); and fruit twice a day. (Tomatoes come under the last heading.) Remember also to serve oily fish such as herring and tinned or fresh salmon occasionally.

Planned meals are much more interesting than those which are haphazard, although you may find it too much of an effort at first to plan meals for a whole week in advance. If you do this, however, you will find it easier to save money and cut your marketing expeditions down to two or three a week. In any case, do try to think out your menus two or three days ahead, although your plans should always be reasonably flexible. When catering for two it is a good scheme sometimes to arrange deliberately to have left-overs. These can be turned into savouries, or may provide the ingredients for an hors d'œuvre. If you cook a double quantity of potatoes on the day you serve them plain boiled, you can use the rest for a salad, croquettes or cakes for the next day. This saves time, fuel and washing-up. Our menu-chart shows how to deal with your day-to-day food "remainders."

The sweet course is often difficult to arrange, especially when your husband is home for lunch as well as dinner. When you are baking a pie, make two or three at a time, filling them with different fruits and mixtures. Serve either hot or cold, with cream, custard or a milk shape, to ring the changes. Learn to make a savoury soufflé. This will not only help you to use up scraps of ham, fish and cheese, but will mean that you can often cut out the sweet course altogether.

Buy a variety of cheeses, too. We are getting the cream of the French cheeses here now, so do not limit your purchases to Cheddar and Cheshire only. Serve (Continued on page 88)

SUNDAY

Dinner
(A) Roast lamb, Mint sauce,
    Peas, Potatoes
Gooseberry tart (hot)
Cream

Supper
Cream cheese and
    Lettuce sandwiches
Cherry trifles

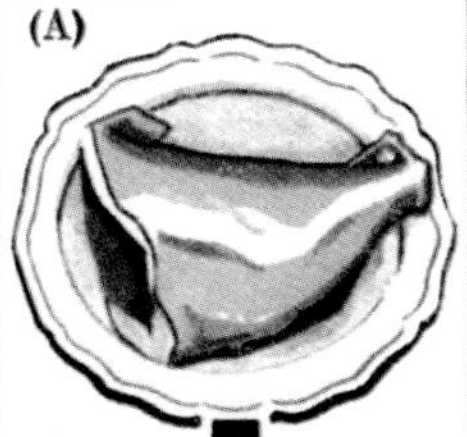

(A)

For economy's sake,
cater so that two or
three dishes may be
based on one pur-
chase, as shown here
in pictorial form

MONDAY

Lunch
Spanish or Onion omelette
Gooseberry tart (cold)
Custard

Dinner
Clear tomato soup
(A) Cold lamb, Salad of peas and
    potatoes
(B) Stewed soft fruits
    Custard

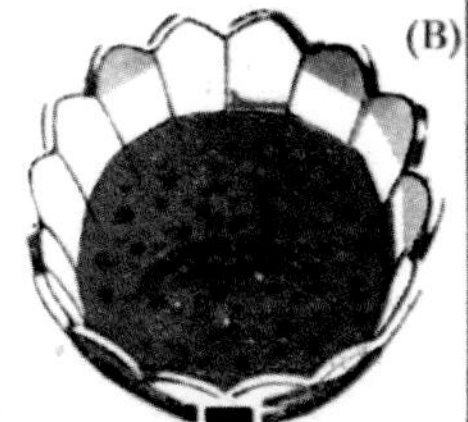

(B)

TUESDAY

Lunch
(A) Cottage pie or Meat rissoles
(B) Summer pudding

Dinner
Kidney stew, Rice
Green vegetables
Cheese soufflé

WEDNESDAY

Lunch
(C) Poached eggs on corn
(C) Sardines on toast

Dinner
Iced melon or Fruit cocktail
(D) Steamed chicken
    Parsley sauce, Mixed vegetables
    Steamed lemon pudding

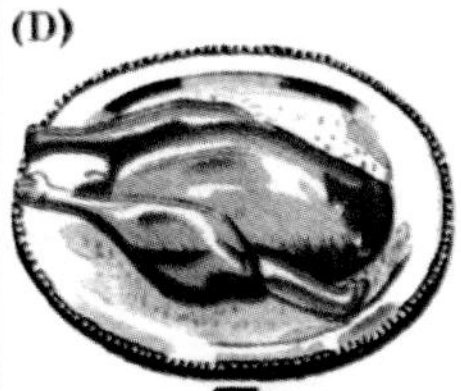

(D)

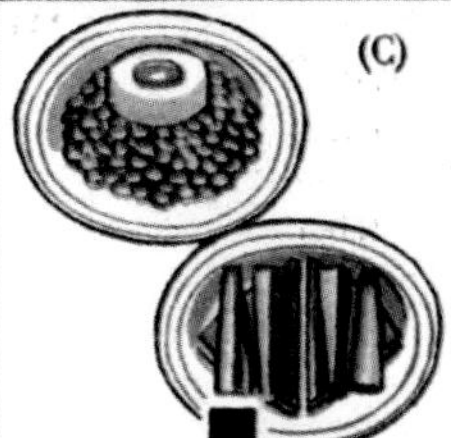

(C)

THURSDAY

Lunch
(D) Chicken (cold), diced, with
    Salad of mixed vegetables
    and lettuce
Compôte of fruit

Dinner
(C) Mixed hors d'œuvre
Oatcakes
Individual fruit tarts

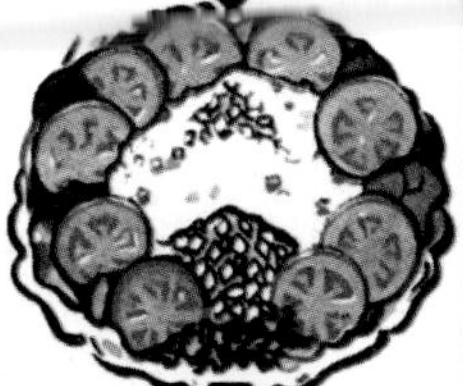

FRIDAY

Lunch
(D) Chicken and ham cutlets
Orange custard

Dinner
Chicken broth, with noodles
(E) Cod cutlets, or Fillets of plaice
Cheese sauce, Tomatoes
Junket and cream

(E)

SATURDAY

Lunch
Raw vegetable salad
Cheese, Wholemeal biscuits
Individual bread, butter and
    raisin puddings

Dinner
(E) Macaroni and fish pie gratinée
Carrots
Baked half-peaches in syrup

To follow up the
history of each group
of dishes above,
look for the corres-
ponding letter in
the menus at left

Good "Buys"

for the holidays and later

"WILL it be practical?" "Will it last?" "Is it the best possible value for the money?" are the questions that determine most of our spending to-day, but while fully admitting their extreme importance, I don't think we should omit a fourth test. When buying clothes, at least, the pleasure they will give us, the uplift to our spirit and morale, ought to be considered, too. After all, if that dress, or coat, or blouse, is going to be our constant companion, in fair weather and rough, for many months, or longer, we'll need to like its face sincerely!

This month, then, while thinking primarily of holidays, I have tried to choose you clothes that will prove good "buys" on every possible score. Take the coats and the suit photographed on page 37, for instance. They're thoroughbreds, and yet not *too* classic. Light enough for travel now, they'll be right way into the winter, and yet when next spring comes round again they will not look a bit dull and heavy.

With holidays in mind I have picked a feather-weight angora slip-on coat : it looks adorable over silk dresses, day or evening, as well as with sports clothes, but you'll find it a real treasure with your winter frocks, too. It comes in the most glorious colours and is a tonic in itself because of this.

Culottes (divided skirts) are a " must " if you cycle, and very practical for all country and in-the-house wear. The ones I choose are made by Gor-ray, the skirt people, and are perfect as to cut and fit. They look like a beautifully balanced, pleated skirt, until you move, and the pleats stay *put* too, as with all Gor-ray styles.

A swim-suit that looks like gleaming velvet is hardly a wartime choice, some of you will say, although I am not sure I agree! If you swim a lot, you'll probably prefer to go slow on something else in order to get a costume as lovely as this one; besides, considering how long it will last, it is compara-

tively inexpensive. Much the same applies to the shorts, which are the new length, full ones, very becoming to those who are no longer slim young girls.

My final good " buy " suggestion (without counting the accessories, which are all extra nice, I think you'll agree), is a lovely heavy, unweighted, pure silk print dress. The design is one of those simple-looking-but-only-available-in-exclusive-qualities conventional ones of which you won't easily tire; the style a compromise between a plain shirt frock and something a little more formal. This is the kind of dress you can wear coatless to a summer wedding or under your winter fur coat

with equally good effect, and it will last and clean like nobody's business !

Next month I hope to give you some budgets to help you with your autumn clothes plan. In the meanwhile don't forget that I am at your service for all and any of your clothes problems. If you have any difficulty in locating the merchan-dise featured in these pages, please write to me direct, enclosing stamped addressed envelope for your reply. I think you will find that most good shops in London and the provinces could get the styles illustrated for you, if they have not already got them in stock.

FRUIT PUNCH

Juice from 1 lb oranges (approx. 1 gill)	1–2 oz. sugar	Ice
Juice from 2 lemons (approx. ½ gill) .	1 pint soda water, or plain water	Mint
	1 pint ginger ale	Grapes
		Sliced lemon

Dissolve the sugar in ¼ pint water and cool. Put the ice into a jug, strain the fruit juice over it, and add the sugar syrup and the bruised mint. Just before serving, add the soda water and ginger ale.

Serve in glasses, and decorate with grapes, thin slices of lemon and sprigs of mint.

Summer's BOUNTY

MUST BE STORED

by E. J. M. Creswell of
the Institute Staff

"TO what extent is it essential to use sugar for jam-making and bottling?" "Can one preserve fruit without using sugar?" "How can surplus vegetables be preserved for winter use?"

These are typical of the questions on fruit and vegetable preservation which the Institute is continually being asked, and which in this article I shall attempt to answer.

While sugar is not essential for bottling, since water can be used instead of syrup, it is, of course, required for jam-making. Even in wartime it is a mistake to reduce the proportion too much, for if you do so your jams will not only set indifferently, but will very likely show signs of fermentation and mould-growth within a few weeks of making.

Substitutes for Sugar

Glucose is now difficult, if not impossible, to obtain, except for medicinal purposes, but if you have saved a small supply, or have stored a certain amount of Golden Syrup or honey, you may be wondering whether these can supplement or replace some of the sugar for your preserves. The uses of these syrups are limited, as, weight for weight, they are less sweet than sugar, and since they contain an appreciable proportion of moisture, they are less concentrated. The effect of substituting them for even 20 to 25 per cent. of the sugar normally used in jam-making is to produce a stickier, tarter preserve, and it is therefore impracticable to attempt using more.

Saccharine is another sweetening agent which may occur to you, but as this has neither preservative nor setting qualities it is useless for jam, other than diabetic preserves where gelatine or another setting agent is used. Also, when in contact with fruit for any length of time it imparts a bitter flavour, so it should only be added at the actual time of serving, whether the fruit is bottled or fresh.

All these ways of bottling fruits, preserving vegetables and making jam have been approved by
THE MINISTRY OF FOOD

If you've grown more beetroot than you need, try turning some of it into beetroot soup

SOUPS

A SUBSTANTIAL soup makes a welcome and nourishing prelude to a meal, or can be served as the main dish for lunch or supper. Good soups were ever the test of the clever housewife, but in these days when every ounce of food, and every penny, has to be used to best advantage, it's up to all of us to rival the Frenchwoman's proverbial skill and economy in soup-making. Here, then, are some recipes you may like to try.

In all of them the quantity of margarine or other fat normally used has been cut down or omitted, and instead of making a roux, the method of blending the thickening agent or liaison with some of the liquid has been adopted. Whole cereals, such as rice or barley, provide a thickening medium that requires no fat. Cream, which greatly improves the texture of thickened soups, must also be omitted at the present time.

Instead of serving the usual fried croûtons, it is a good plan to cut spare pieces of bread or crusts into neat pieces and dry them in the oven until lightly brown. These can then be served with any soup.

Beetroot Soup

1 lb. cooked beetroot	2 teaspoonfuls cornflour
½ pint stock	Few drops lemon juice or
¼ pint milk	vinegar
Salt and pepper	Carmine or cochineal

Skin and slice the beetroot and put it into a saucepan with the stock. Simmer about 15 minutes, until the beetroot is very soft, then pass through a sieve. Blend the cornflour with the milk and add to the beetroot. Bring to the boil, stirring well, and cook two or three minutes. Add salt and pepper and a little red colouring, if necessary. Lastly add a few drops of lemon juice or vinegar.

If preferred, raw beetroots may be used for this soup, in which case they should be washed and peeled before cooking, as it is unnecessary to prevent them bleeding. They should be sliced and cooked in the stock until tender—two or three hours.

Brussels Sprout Purée

½ lb. sprouts	¼ pint milk
1 pint stock	½ oz. flour
	Salt and pepper

Boil the sprouts until quite tender,

This celery soup is thick, smooth and full of flavour, with its seasoning and grated cheese

Particularly popular with the menfolk is kidney soup—warming, nourishing and savoury

you'll enjoy

then drain, and rub them through a hair sieve. Add them to the stock and bring to the boil. Blend the flour with the milk, add to the soup and allow to boil two or three minutes, stirring continuously. Season with salt and pepper.

Celery Soup

1 head celery	½ pint milk
1 onion	1 oz. rice
¾ pint stock	Salt and pepper
Bouquet garni	1 oz. cheese, if liked

Wash and slice the celery and put it in a stewpan with the stock, well washed rice and sliced onion. Add the bouquet garni, tied in muslin, and a little salt and pepper. Simmer about

an hour, then remove the bouquet garni and pass the soup through a sieve. Add the milk and a little grated cheese, if liked, and reheat before serving.

Milk Soup

This is a basic recipe for a quickly made milk soup, and may be varied by the substitution or addition of other flavouring vegetables and herbs that may be available, e.g. turnips, carrot, etc.

1 pint milk	1 oz. margarine
1 onion	1 oz. flour
Stalk of celery	1 oz. cheese
2 cloves	½ teaspoonful chopped
Blade of mace	parsley
	Salt and pepper

Put the milk in a saucepan with the sliced onion, celery, cloves and mace and simmer very gently for about ½ hour, taking care that the milk is not allowed to boil over or burn. Strain, and leave on one side (the vegetables removed may be put into the stock-pot). Taking the same saucepan, melt the margarine and stir in the flour. Add the flavoured milk by degrees and bring to the boil, stirring continuously. Cook two or three minutes, then add the cheese and season carefully. Pour into a hot soup tureen or individual soup cups, and sprinkle with chopped parsley before serving.

Kidney Soup

¾ lb. ox kidney	¼ teaspoonful pepper
1 quart stock	1 tablespoonful chopped
2 oz. dripping	onion
2 oz. flour	1 carrot
½ teaspoonful salt	Slice of turnip
	Bunch of herbs

Cut the kidney into very small pieces and toss *(Continued on page* 77)

Brussels Sprout Purée is one of the less common but very good vegetable soups

HECTOR BOLITHO has never had

THE FUTURE

"To my mind, a great leader must possess three great ism . . . I do not think that I need speak to you about its keynote is personal contact and understanding . . . lead unless he has the gift of vision and the desire in he found them."

QUIET thinking is not easy during a war. But there are lulls in which most of us wonder over the future—imagining what form our lives will take when the horror drifts away. There are some who believe that Monarchy will come back to Europe, and they talk of Germany being broken into small states, with lesser princes returned to their thrones. It may seem an over-optimistic picture for monarchists to draw, when we look towards Europe now and see the plight in which contemporary sovereigns find themselves. King Carol, who was a good domestic ruler, was forced from his throne by the powers of the Axis, and young King Michael is the pathetic and powerless guardian of a dynasty which seems to have a very shaky future. King Leopold's fate is wrapped in mystery. The fine old King of Denmark is more or less a prisoner in his own country. The King of Norway and the Queen of the Netherlands are exiles in England, keeping the little flame of their countries' pride alive: waiting for better days. The King of Italy is overburdened by the ridiculous and dangerous figure of his dictator.

The fortunes of princes in Europe are indeed lower than they have ever been before. But in this country and the Empire, monarchy stands as high as ever, and while the eclipse of the European sovereigns is almost complete, our own King and Queen rise to greater and greater heights of influence: like a spirit behind the law: an example and an inspiration. I heard a great man say of the King and Queen a little time ago, "They have the rare talent of being able to make a mass of people realise, in a flash, that they are good." This sentence bears close examination. It is this quality of goodness which is of double value to us now, when it seems that human nature is so corrupted by war that we have to struggle to keep our faith alive.

The mystery may have gone out of kingship. It is true that its functions have changed, so that a king commands our loyalty through his own character rather than by his power. But this personal influence is far greater when he is the keeper rather than the maker of the law. This has been proved so splendidly during the past year and a half of the war. From a modest beginning, these two "good" people have come to represent a standard to us—they hold a looking-glass up to the best that is in us, and we are comforted by their existence. Not so very long ago, when the King was in the East End, somebody called out to him, "You are a great King." He answered, "And you are a great people." We should be proud of that! It makes the kind of leadership which tortures Europe seem vulgar, cruel and destructive, by comparison.

History is repeating itself. It was the war of 1914–18 that brought King George V and Queen Mary near to the people. This war is bringing the young King and Queen equally near, and we don't have to pretend or shake up old shibboleths to tell this truth to the world.

But it is surprising that so few people remember, or realise, that King George VI is a pilot and almost a veteran in warfare. He is the first king in our history who is a qualified pilot of the Royal Air Force. It is

a better subject than this . . .

OF MONARCHY

qualities: personality, sympathy and, above all, ideal-
personality . . . Of sympathy I will just say this . . .
the third quality of the leader is idealism. Nobody can
his soul to leave things in the world a little better than
H.M. the King, in his first speech.

not an empty ceremony when he puts on his blue uniform, with wings over his heart. They are there because
he earned them.

I have talked to the officer who taught the King to
fly. He said to me, "He had the rare quality which an
instructor always dreams of instilling into his pupil. By
instinct he was able to use eyes, hands and brain in
unison—he was amazingly quick. He seemed to know
where he had his aeroplane in relation to the ground
without any trouble."

There are people at Windsor who remember the day
when the King made his first solo flight over the Castle.
It is romantic now to realise that the young pilot who
flew over the home of his ancestors now walks up the
hill at Windsor, as King.

It is important, when we see photographs of the King
in the newspapers, presenting decorations to the pilots
of the Royal Air Force, to remember that it means a
great deal to them to receive their medal at the hands
of a sovereign who understands their work and who
watches the progress of the battle in the air with real
knowledge and experience.

But we must also remember that the King served in
the last war with the Navy, and that he took part in the
Battle of Jutland. Some years ago I talked to an officer
who was with him in the turret on the great day of the
battle. For some minutes during the action the King—
then Prince Albert—climbed on to the top of the turret
and watched the battle: a distinctly daring thing to do.
He saw the *Marlborough* hit by a torpedo five hundred
yards away, and another torpedo approaching his own
ship on the starboard side. But Prince Albert's moment
came when a German shell struck the water some yards
off the ship and ricochetted over the turret on which he
was standing. The officer told me that Prince Albert
had to duck his head to miss it. He hurried back into
the turret, and his senior officer said, "What the hell's
the matter with you?" He answered, "I'm coming
down now, sir."

Remembering this story, and the fact that the King is
a qualified pilot, gives added value to what he is doing
now. I thought of this on the day when he broadcast
after the bombing of Buckingham Palace: when he
spoke of its "honourable scars." He didn't seem to be
a young King any longer.

We read a great deal about the purpose of this war.
Hitler has his philosophy in a nutshell. And some people
seem to think that we ought to be able to express our
aims in a phrase. It is not as simple as that. But I
think that the life of the King and Queen at the present
time is a symbol of those aims.

The King once made a remarkable speech. It was
his first, and he wrote it himself when he was about
eighteen. He said:

"To my mind, a great leader must possess three
great qualities: personality, sympathy and, above all,
idealism. . . . I do not think that I need speak to you
about personality. . . . Of sympathy I will just say
this . . . its keynote is (*Continued on page* **70**)

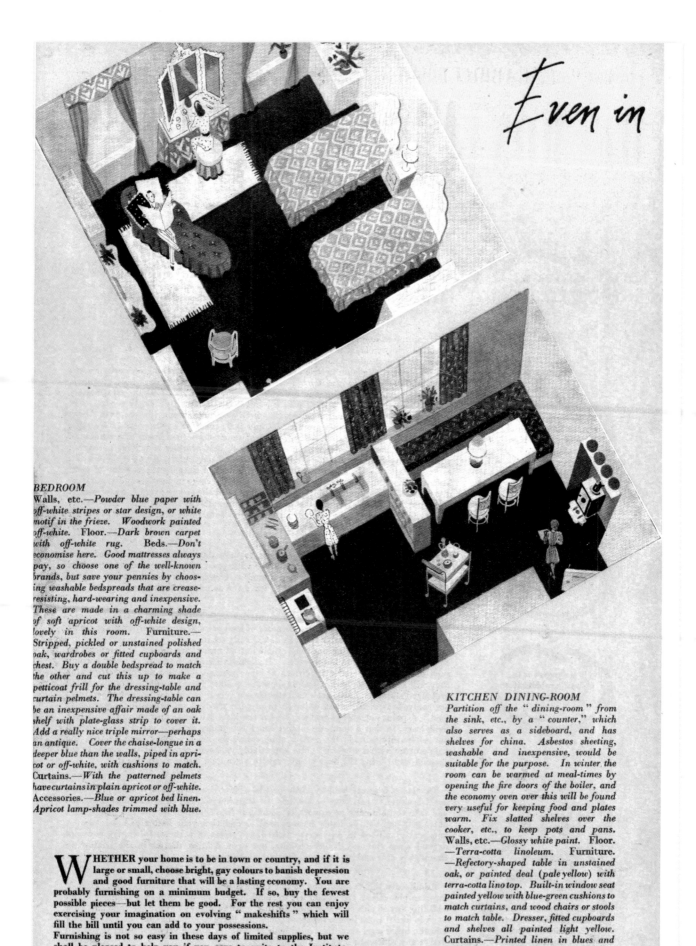

BEDROOM

Walls, etc.—*Powder blue paper with off-white stripes or star design, or white motif in the frieze. Woodwork painted off-white.* Floor.—*Dark brown carpet with off-white rug.* Beds.—*Don't economise here. Good mattresses always pay, so choose one of the well-known brands, but save your pennies by choosing washable bedspreads that are crease-resisting, hard-wearing and inexpensive. These are made in a charming shade of soft apricot with off-white design, lovely in this room.* Furniture.—*Stripped, pickled or unstained polished oak, wardrobes or fitted cupboards and chest. Buy a double bedspread to match the other and cut this up to make a petticoat frill for the dressing-table and curtain pelmets. The dressing-table can be an inexpensive affair made of an oak shelf with plate-glass strip to cover it. Add a really nice triple mirror—perhaps an antique. Cover the chaise-longue in a deeper blue than the walls, piped in apricot or off-white, with cushions to match.* Curtains.—*With the patterned pelmets have curtains in plain apricot or off-white.* Accessories.—*Blue or apricot bed linen. Apricot lamp-shades trimmed with blue.*

KITCHEN DINING-ROOM

Partition off the "dining-room" from the sink, etc., by a "counter," which also serves as a sideboard, and has shelves for china. Asbestos sheeting, washable and inexpensive, would be suitable for the purpose. In winter the room can be warmed at meal-times by opening the fire doors of the boiler, and the economy oven over this will be found very useful for keeping food and plates warm. Fix slatted shelves over the cooker, etc., to keep pots and pans. Walls, etc.—*Glossy white paint.* Floor. —*Terra-cotta linoleum.* Furniture. —*Refectory-shaped table in unstained oak, or painted deal (pale yellow) with terra-cotta lino top. Built-in window seat painted yellow with blue-green cushions to match curtains, and wood chairs or stools to match table. Dresser, fitted cupboards and shelves all painted light yellow.* Curtains.—*Printed linen in blues and greens on a natural ground.* Accessories. —*Oatmeal and green kitchenware, etc.*

WHETHER your home is to be in town or country, and if it is large or small, choose bright, gay colours to banish depression and good furniture that will be a lasting economy. You are probably furnishing on a minimum budget. If so, buy the fewest possible pieces—but let them be good. For the rest you can enjoy exercising your imagination on evolving "makeshifts" which will fill the bill until you can add to your possessions.

Furnishing is not so easy in these days of limited supplies, but we shall be pleased to help you if you care to write to the Institute.

"200 Household Hints," price 7½d. post free, is a mine of information on domestic problems of all kinds.

Wartime People must Furnish —

by Elizabeth White
of the Institute Staff

LIVING-ROOM
Walls, etc.—Cream matt finish paint. Floor.—A fitted carpet will add to your comfort and guards against draughts. Choose a deep blue crush-resisting carpeting which will not show footmarks. Furniture.—At least two low, roomy arm-chairs and settee of modern design. Have them upholstered in grey with a touch of black. We should like a few pieces of old or reproduction mahogany furniture here—you may pick these up at a dealer's or auction-rooms, or in the second-hand department of a London store. Curtains.—For economy choose curtains suitable for all the year round. We suggest apricot or flame-coloured velvet. Lined with casement or sateen, and made amply full to hang well above the window, they will also serve for black-out. Lighting.—Wall brackets, say on either side of the fireplace and two on the opposite wall, with a standard lamp, make a pleasing lighting scheme.

See page 74 for details of these furnishings.

"Summertime Recipe Book," price 7½d. post free, will prove invaluable during the warmer months.

Tested and Approved
SERIAL Nº
GOOD HOUSEKEEPING INSTITUTE
LONDON
Conducted by
GOOD HOUSEKEEPING MAGAZINE

Good Housekeeping
Institute presents **News**

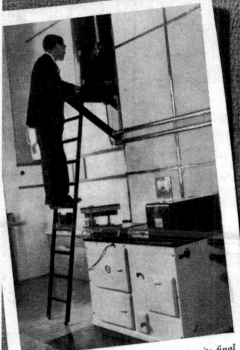

The A.B. cooker is seen here undergoing its final water- and oven-heating tests. The Institute engineer is reading the temperature of the water

By P. L. Garbutt, A.I.C.

First Class Diploma King's College
of Household and Social Science;
late staff Battersea Polytechnic

DURING the three months which have elapsed since our last Bulletin was published the Institute has been having a very busy time. Food, we realise, is still one of the main problems of the day, and now that so many articles are temporarily scarce and difficult to obtain, it is not always easy to answer the ever-recurring question, "What shall we have for breakfast, dinner or supper?" "Good Housekeeping" sixpenny series of cookery books (7½d. post free) will help you with this difficult part of your housekeeping, which these days often involves a quick change in plans, according to the result of the morning's shopping. Among them you will find ideas for wartime meals and suggestions for those days when you have consumed your meat ration for the week and it is not easy to think of a nourishing and attractive substitute for the main dish. Needless to say, the recipes have all been tried out in the kitchens of Good Housekeeping Institute, and between them these books form a useful wartime cooking library. The books which are now available or will shortly be ready include:

New Wartime Recipes
Vegetarian and Casserole Recipes (revised edition shortly available)
Unusual Vegetables—How to Grow and How to Cook Them
Cakes and Puddings for Wartime
Book of Wartime Preserves

By the way, you should make a note of the Preserve Book referred to last. This will be found invaluable during the coming months, when every effort must be made to save and conserve as much fruit as possible for winter use, and this with the minimum possible amount of sugar. We have therefore concentrated on reduced sugar jams, jellies and marmalades, as well as including a section dealing with fruit bottling and pickling. Vegetable preservation is also discussed, though lack of natural acidity and sugar makes sterilisation with ordinary home equipment much more difficult than is the case with fruit. However, there are certain safe methods, and full directions will be found in this publication.

Onions and Lemons

At the time of writing, onions and lemons are both practically unobtainable, and so we have been very glad to test useful substitutes for these in the Institute kitchens. These are Unyun Condiment and Lem-Lem. Excellent results were obtained with the former, provided the powder was added to dishes such as casseroles and stews only just before serving. Needless to say, care must also be taken with such a volatile type of product to replace the lid of the carton immediately after use.

Lemon juice, of course, consists essentially of dilute citric acid, and is also valuable on account of its vitamin C content. Lem-Lem powder, diluted according to the instructions supplied with it, gives a liquid of similar acidity and vitamin content, and one which can replace lemon juice for cooking purposes. For marmalade and jams, for instance, requiring lemon juice to improve their flavour and setting qualities,

Miss Ramsay of the Institute staff ascertains the average oven temperatures of the New World stove which correspond to the different Regulo settings

Bulletin №3

Tested and Approved
SERIAL №
GOOD HOUSEKEEPING INSTITUTE
LONDON
Conducted by
GOOD HOUSEKEEPING MAGAZINE

Tested products and appliances referred to in this article may be obtained from Good Housekeeping Centre

Lem-Lem is an extremely useful product and one of which we have made extensive use when preparing recipes for the *Good Housekeeping Book of Wartime Preserves,* which is now available.

Cookery research during the last few months has indeed provided us with a number of worth-while wartime recipes, including one for lemon curd, using Lem-Lem in the place of fresh lemons, and some new ways of utilising tinned foods such as crawfish. The following are recipes which have won special approval from the Institute staff.

Mock Lemon Curd

1 oz. margarine	1 heaped teaspoonful cornflour
¼ lb. sugar	1 egg
¾ teaspoonful Lem-Lem powder	Orange essence

Place margarine, sugar, Lem-Lem and three tablespoonfuls water in a double saucepan, and bring to boiling-point. Blend the cornflour with ¼ gill cold water, stir into the mixture, and cook for about 10 minutes. Add the beaten egg, stir well, and cook for 5 minutes. Add 3–4 drops orange essence. Pot and cover as usual.

Cape Crawfish Casserole

2 small tins (or 1 large tin) Cape Crawfish	¼ pint shelled green peas
1 onion or 6 spring onions	Seasoning
A few young carrots	1–2 oz. soft breadcrumbs
	1 oz. margarine (melted)

Peel and slice the onion, scrape and slice the carrots. Put the vegetables in a saucepan with seasoning and a little water and cook until tender. Drain and reserve the liquor and with it make a cream sauce (see directions below). Divide the crawfish into small pieces, combine with the peas, carrots and onion, and add the sauce. Turn into a casserole and cover with the breadcrumbs. Sprinkle the top with a little melted margarine and bake in a moderate oven until lightly brown, about 20 minutes.

N.B.—If you should have difficulty in obtaining supplies of Cape Crawfish, you can, if necessary, substitute other canned or fresh fish in this recipe.

Cream Sauce

½ pint mixed milk and liquor from vegetables	1½ oz. flour
	Piece of margarine
	Seasoning

Blend the flour with a little of the liquor. Heat the rest, then add the blended flour and stir until boiling. Season, and beat in a nut of margarine. Simmer for a few minutes, then use as directed above.

Before leaving the question of food, readers may like to have their attention drawn to a very readable little volume on diet entitled *Healthy Eating,* by Professor V. H. Mottram (Cassell, 3s.). Professor Mottram has some scathing remarks for the food crank, and stresses the importance of an all-round, common-sense dietary, which can be assured even in wartime.

(*Continued on page* 86)

Cape Crawfish Casserole and Lemon Meringue Tarts using a mock lemon curd are two particularly successful recipes we have evolved recently

Here is Miss Creswell at work in the Cookery Research Kitchen, trying out recipes for one of our 6d. series of Wartime Cookery Books

Salute to the WRENS

CICELY FRASER *visits Greenwich, and comes away genuinely impressed.*

GREENWICH is nearer to London than I remembered, and the way there took me through a series of rather squalid neighbourhoods. But when I had passed through the gates of the Royal Naval College, where the W.R.N.S. has its depôt and O.T.C., a wind blew in from the sea with a salty tang, and two seagulls called harshly to each other. The picture was completed when, looking through an archway which a moment before had shown nothing but blank horizon, I saw the funnels of a passing cargo ship silhouetted against the sky. And I thought to myself that if I were one of the girls who pass through that gateway for the period of probationary training which is their farewell to civilian life, I should have taken these signs as a welcome into the Navy. I thought, too, when I had seen the College, that a place so bound up with English history, with so very definite an atmosphere, must mean something to those who train there. It must help them to realise that they are entering a Service with a mighty heritage.

The Wrens cheerfully admit that when their organisation was started during the 1914–18 war, many sailors viewed its appearance with horror. The Senior Service, the Silent Service, had been a masculine stronghold as sacrosanct as Law or Church up till then. But it did not take the women long to prove their worth, and, once admitted, the Navy treated them generously. When this war broke out the W.R.N.S. received a warm welcome.

Before going down to Greenwich I had already paid a couple of visits to the London headquarters of the service and had the chance of talking to some of the people in command there. One of the things that struck me was the fact that the Wrens take great care—unusual care, from my knowledge of other government and national organisations—to fit people into jobs for which they are really suited.

First-officer Samuel described to me how all applicants for the Service are given a personal interview, where they are encouraged to discuss their qualifications.

"We put no one into work for which she has not applied. If a girl wants to join as a clerk, and there are no vacancies, we tell her so. We do not accept her and then turn her willy-nilly into a cook."

From this interview a dossier of the applicant is prepared. If she joins the W.R.N.S. this will follow her wherever she goes, with constant additions as her time of service goes on. At any moment, therefore, if promotion is in question, her

officers will know exactly how far any individual is ready for a move up.

Every opportunity is given to a girl to select her future job. An applicant may come with no very clear idea of what she could do, I was told.

"She may be someone who has lived at home, doing some housework perhaps, but not very much else, and with no business training. In that case she might find a post as a steward, where her knowledge of how to lay and decorate a table, and her experience of how food should be served, would make her a valuable assistant at an officers' mess. Or there are girls of the type who came here recently, who said she was an absolute fool at everything. But it turned out that she could not only drive a car but also a motor-cycle, and she is now a most useful dispatch rider."

I was interested to hear also of the treatment accorded to another class of applicant, the older woman, who has already occupied some administrative position.

"We always have room for them," said First-Officer Samuel. "We appreciate the fact that in many cases they are giving up a good living to join us because they want to help the country, and though they have to begin as ratings, like everyone else, they will have little difficulty in being promoted to officers—providing, of course, that they live up to our expectations of them. One woman gave up a practice as a solicitor, and she now has a most responsible position in the W.R.N.S. Others have had experience in social service, and make excellent officers in charge of the girls at the ports. And, of course, there are numerous posts which must be occupied by women with high secretarial and business qualifications—accountancy jobs, work connected with supplies and storage."

One of the worst things about modern war is the way in which it chops years from the lives of those engaged in it, giving no return. The W.R.N.S. (Continued on page 44)

● THESE photographs give a cross-section of W.R.N.S. activities. You see girls receiving individual tuition during their nine-weeks' course at a Royal Naval Cookery School; dispatch riders returning to H.Q.; a Wren doing clerical work at a Royal Naval Barracks; others embarking on a tender for the training ship where they work as stewards and writers; members of the O.T.C. dining in the painted hall at the Royal Naval College, Greenwich; and two typical groups of officers and of Wrens.

By Margaret Pulsford

Marry me so that I have the right to belong to you

After the war . . .

You mean you don't want to marry me?

LOVE *must*

MERRIL woke up in the small bedroom which smelt of sea salt. There was no sound except the demanding cry of the gulls and the slow boom-boom of the waves against the rocks.

Drowsily her thoughts wandered back to the beginning of Larry's leave, the leave which was to have been the whole fabric of happiness for them, but which had brought little but strain and heartbreak.

She knew on the instant of meeting that something was lost between them. She could tell by the way he kissed her. The old natural harmony was gone. He was tense, restless and, what hurt most, wary.

"Let's have a good time, Merril," he said, "a rousing one. Get the gang together. I want to see people, lots of them."

At first she tried to argue that this was natural. Everyone said a man on leave wanted to go about and hear talk and music. It helped them to forget the war, specially a man like Larry, fresh from the strain of night flying in enemy skies.

So they packed the days with parties and noise, or he went off on his own, and disappointment piled up inside her until she felt as if tears were running down her heart. Because she soon realised it was no good arguing. He wanted parties and people because he did not want to be alone with her. It was his way of showing he no longer wanted to marry her.

Then, suddenly coming home in a taxi with him one evening before a week of his leave was over, she knew she could stand it no more. Covertly, in the dim light, she stole a look at him. She could see only the black outline of his profile, abbreviated because of the peak of his service cap, but because it was still and averted it told her everything. In the old days he would have been turned to her, eager not to miss a single expression on her face.

Yet if the Air Force had not swallowed him up with a sudden twenty-four hours' notice to report for duty, she would have been married to him by now for six months. She tried to console herself that then the tragedy would have been greater, but it did not answer the eternal question in her mind: "What had happened?" And, once again her thoughts began their despairing circling inside her head, hoping to avoid the conclusion it was because he no longer loved her. But she knew it was useless and it was at that moment she decided it was no good pretending any more. She must hear the sentence from his own lips. Only then could she really accept it.

For a fleeting moment she thought of the dress hanging up in the cupboard and the big-brimmed hat to match because he always said: "Darling, I do like a hat to be a hat, not something the size of a gaudy peanut." These were to have been her wedding garments, because, before their hurried parting six months ago, Larry said:

"It won't mean we'll have to wait long, sweetheart. I'm sure to get leave pretty soon. Then we'll make up for everything with a special licence."

So, while he was being turned into a pilot and became acquainted with death and the icy, lonely thrill of danger, she dreamed of his first leave and, when his wire came, rushed out madly to buy the dress and hat.

She knew now she would never wear them and, with odd inconsequence, thought of the dressmaker who had rushed herself to a pitch of frenzy to get the dress finished in time. "She'll be mad it was all for nothing," Merril thought with the ghost of a grin.

As the taxi stopped outside her door, she said:

"Come up for a few minutes, Larry. I want to talk to you."

Her words sounded stilted and also timid. She who had always felt so close to him was now afraid of a rebuff.

"All right," he said, "but I can't stop long, darling. I feel whacked to the wide."

She knew he did not want to come. It had been the same all through those heartbreaking days, the fear of being alone with her.

When he lighted a cigarette for her and was putting a match to his own, she said:

"You don't want to marry me, do you, Larry?"

after the war . . .

You mean you have not stopped loving me?

I might be maimed and then you'd be saddled with me

Illustration by Ernest Ratcliffe

not WAIT

He looked away from her and everything about her seemed to go still. Her body felt a hollow place which housed nothing but her beating heart.

"No, Merril."

Even her heart stopped then as if it wished to be a silent spectator while her love was told to go. By a tremendous effort she managed not to change the expression on her face and said:

"I had to know. I had to ask. We've been a bit silly, haven't we. You should have told me at once."

But her voice, unsteady and full of tears, was an agony which humiliated her. It was not right it should betray her. He should think that she felt as he did. Only when he was gone should her grief reveal itself.

Suddenly he was close to her, holding her elbows firmly in the palms of his hands.

"You don't understand," he said. "I mean I don't want to marry you now. Not until after the war."

Her head felt light and every nerve pricked coldly in her body from the shock of the reprieve.

"You mean you haven't stopped loving me?"

"You thought that? Oh, Merril!"

He kissed her, and with the kiss they found each other again and afterwards they stood for a moment close together, holding hands, each finding new knowledge of the other, silently, deeply, as children do.

At last she asked:

"But why do you want to wait, Larry?" and felt at once the spell between them break and the tense, nervousness return to him.

He stepped away from her and said with difficulty:

"Because it wouldn't be fair to you. You see, nobody minds getting killed, but I might be maimed and then you'd be saddled with me. I couldn't stand it."

"Nobody minds getting killed," the brave pity of the words woke such a passionate protectiveness in her she wanted to fling her arms around him and hold him close. But she knew he would hate that. Besides, it would do no good. This was the moment when she must fight for the happiness that alone he was afraid to take.

She argued, as women have argued through the centuries:

"But we'd still have each other. We'd still love each other. Nothing could change that."

And, as she spoke, her heart wept and called to him to understand. She wanted to say: "Don't you see that if you were helpless I'd love you even more. I'd slave for you. It isn't the body that matters. It's you I want. Why should you think that because I'd be what you call free, I'd be happy. I love you. I'll never be free again. For pity's sake marry me so that I have the right to belong to you."

But she knew, of course, she could not say such things. He would be shocked and embarrassed. He would be so cornered he might yield out of pity. And that was the one way she would not have him.

He said: "You say that now, darling, and bless you for it. But I've had time to do some thinking, and I know that if I do get smashed up, it'll be more tolerable for me if you are free."

She wanted to cry: "Always yourself. Always yourself and your man's pride," but she said quietly:

"Anything that happens to you will be more tolerable for me if I'm your wife."

But she knew it was hopeless and, when he held her in his arms, the will to argue went out of her. She knew only the eternal, the elemental desire to yield to him.

"After the war, Merril, after the war," he said, and being close to him again softened her sense of loss and made her feel that perhaps after all it would not be so hard to wait.

As if reading her thoughts he said:

"Isn't it wonderful to be like this again, close! I've hated the past few days, but I didn't know how to go about things, how to tell you so that you wouldn't be hurt."

And she marvelled, as many women have done, at the queer conviction men have that the last thing they should do is speak their innermost thoughts to a woman with directness. But all she said was:

"Now we've got things settled, let's drop these silly parties. Let's go into the country (*Continued on page* 42)

A careless driver to-day may be a murderer to-morrow.

FIGHTER-STATION W.A.A.Fs.

I HAD always imagined that life on a Fighter Station would be lived among the incessant droning of 'planes. But it was not until I had spent some hours there that the familiar throbbing sounded in the sky. Then, looking through the Georgian bay windows of what was once a country house, I watched a squadron of fighter 'planes returning home from an "offensive sweep." They flew in perfect V formation, losing height as they came, and eventually circling easily towards the landing-ground, which, with the hangars and workshops of the Station, lay nearby behind the house.

At the sound of their engines heads popped out of windows to watch them come in.

"We never get tired of seeing them go off and return," said a W.A.A.F. officer. "The girls will spend half their lunch-hours looking on at the landing-ground."

"It helps us to remember that we are part of the Air Force, and that's always a thrill," said an eighteen-year-old W.A.A.F. in confirmation.

Country houses, however picturesque (and this one is still picturesque, in spite of its ugly camouflage) are not ideal for accommodating large numbers of Air Force personnel. The W.A.A.F. had to *(Continued on page 90)*

(Continued on page 90)

In this Operations Room girl plotters translate messages from R.A.F. and W.A.A.F. radiolocator operators into visible form on a table map. Other W.A.A.F. activities are glimpsed in the smaller pictures

After commissioning the article opposite on Douglas Bader, we thought it would be a good idea to show how the W.A.A.F. backs up our fighter pilots, so here is the thrilling inside story of the women of a Fighter Station, told by CICELY FRASER

National Wheatmeal flour gives these Scotch Pancakes, Biscuits and Scones a delicious nutty flavour

Do You Know How to Use Wheatmeal Flour?

By N. H. Ramsay
of the Institute
Staff

THE National Wheatmeal Loaf is now well known, and liked, but you may not be so familiar with the flour from which it is made, although this is now available for general use. It contains 85 per cent. of the whole wheat berry, and because of this it is rich in vitamin B complex and in certain valuable salts which are lacking in super-refined white flour.

It is up to all of us to use this flour more extensively, to build up our restricted war-time diet, and—equally important—to save space in our ships crossing the Atlantic. If your grocer has not got it in stock, ask him to get it for you. Remember, supply creates demand, and by making every effort to obtain it yourself, you will make it easier for other people to buy it, too.

National Wheatmeal Flour has been used extensively in Good Housekeeping kitchens, and we should like all our readers to try it out in their cooking, for we have found it excellent. Cakes and puddings made with it have a particularly pleasant flavour and an attractive appearance, and it also gives an added richness to biscuits and pastry.

Sea Pie is an old favourite, which tastes even better when made with Wheatmeal flour

Sea Pie

(Filling)

¾ to 1 lb. stewing steak or neck of mutton	4 oz. beans or split peas
1 onion or leek	About 1 pint stock or water
2 or 3 carrots	Freshly ground black pepper
1 turnip	
Stick of celery	Salt
	1 oz. wheatmeal flour

(Wheatmeal Crust)

8 oz. wheatmeal flour	2 oz. suet
Salt and pepper	Cold water
¼ teaspoonful baking powder	

Soak the beans or peas overnight, with a pinch of soda bicarbonate added to the water. Cut the meat in neat pieces, and mix with fresh vegetables, cut in dice or sliced. Mix the wheatmeal flour with the salt and black pepper. Fill a casserole or saucepan with layers of meat, diced vegetables and beans, sprinkle with the seasoned flour, then pour on liquid till the mixture is barely covered.

Make the crust by mixing the flour, seasoning, baking powder and suet and adding enough water to make a light dough. Roll out 1-in. smaller than the size of the casserole or saucepan. Bring meat and vegetables to the boil, then place the crust on top, cover with a close-fitting lid and simmer for 2½ hours.

When ready cut the crust in triangular slices like a cake, and serve the stew in the casserole.

Scotch Pancakes

8 oz. wheatmeal flour	1 oz. melted fat
¼ teaspoonful salt	Approximately ¼ pint milk or water to mix
1½ teaspoonfuls baking powder	
1 teaspoonful sugar	

Sieve the dry ingredients. Melt the fat. Make a well in the centre of the dry ingredients and blend in the liquid smoothly, adding sufficient to make a thick, creamy batter, then stir in the

Safeguard Britain's stocks of food—Kill Master Rat and all his brood.

May there be—

Peace in your Heart
this Christmas-tide.
We offer Greetings to you and
all your loved ones,
wherever they may be.

Drawings by Tage Werner

Holiday Catering, 1941

We can't be lavish this Christmas, and we mustn't mind abandoning some of our traditional dishes, but we can make the most of what we have. Here we suggest a scheme to help you—especially those who have not had to undertake it before—to plan and carry out your Christmas catering with ease and success

THE DAYS BEFORE . . .

Remember that smooth running depends on careful planning, so decide on the menu and order the stores in good time. Plan and prepare the decorations, too, so that you are not rushed at the last moment.

● The cake, pudding and mincemeat, being less rich than usual, should not be made more than one or two weeks in advance. Incidentally, if one variety of fruit is not available, substitute a rather larger proportion of one of the others, if you have sufficient. Here are the recipes we suggest:

Wartime Christmas Cake

½ lb. flour	¼ lb. currants
¼ teaspoonful salt	¼ lb. sultanas
4 oz. fat	¼ lb. raisins (if available)
4 oz. sugar	
½ teaspoonful mixed spice	1 oz. mixed peel (if available)
¼ teaspoonful bicarbonate of soda	1 or 2 eggs
	Milk to mix

Stone and chop the raisins; wash, dry and pick the currants and sultanas; chop the peel. Cream the fat and sugar together very thoroughly, until light and creamy in texture. Add the beaten egg by degrees, mixing very well, and adding a little of the flour if the mixture appears to curdle. Add the prepared fruits, and lastly the flour, salt, spice and bicarbonate of soda, adding enough milk to make the mixture of a dropping consistency. Put into a greased, lined cake tin about 6 to 7 in. in diameter, and bake in a slow oven at a temperature of about 325° F. for from 3 to 4 hours.

Wartime Christmas Pudding

½ lb. flour and breadcrumbs mixed	¼ lb. sultanas
¼ lb. suet	¼ lb. home-dried plums or apple rings
¼ teaspoonful salt	
½ teaspoonful mixed spice	1 oz. mixed peel (if available)
Little grated nutmeg	1 egg
A pinch of ground ginger	Approximately ¼ pint milk
2 oz. sugar	A little caramel to colour
¼ lb. currants	

Wash, dry and pick the currants and sultanas. Chop the peel and the dried plums or apple rings. Mix together the flour and breadcrumbs, suet, salt, sugar and spices. Add the prepared fruit, and mix with the beaten egg and milk to make of a soft dropping consistency, colouring with a little caramel. Put into a greased basin, cover with greased paper and a cloth, and steam or boil for about 6 to 7 hours. Cover with a clean cloth, and store in a cool, dry place until required.

Wartime Mincemeat

¼ lb. currants	¼ lb. carrot
¼ lb sultanas	¼ lb. apple (weighed after peeling)
¼ lb. raisins (if available)	3 oz. suet
2 oz. mixed peel (if available)	½ teaspoonful mixed spice
3 oz. sugar	

Prepare the fruits in the following way: wash, dry and pick the currants and sultanas, and stone the raisins, if used. Peel and core the apples, and scrape the carrot. Put all these, together with the peel and suet, through the mincer, and mix well together. Add the sugar and spice, and stir for a few moments. Cover, and keep in a cool, dry place, stirring every day for about a week. Put into clean, dry jam-jars, cover as for jam, and use as required.

This mincemeat should be used within 2 or 3 weeks, as it is likely to ferment if kept for longer.

ON CHRISTMAS EVE . . . .

● To avoid a last-minute rush, much of the cooking can be prepared on Christmas Eve. Make the stuffing, stuff and truss the bird, and leave ready for roasting. Prepare crumbs, etc., for bread sauce. Stew giblets for gravy. The stuffing can be made with sausage meat or chestnuts, or may be a breadcrumb forcemeat flavoured with herbs.

● Make and bake the mince pies, and while the oven is still warm cook the biscuits. Here is a good recipe:

Chocolate Short Biscuits

3½ oz. wheatmeal flour	2 oz. margarine
	2 oz. sugar
½ oz. cocoa or chocolate powder	A very little cold water
¼ teaspoonful baking powder	A few drops vanilla essence
A pinch of salt	

Mix together the flour, cocoa, salt and baking powder, and rub in the fat very thoroughly until it completely disappears. Then add the sugar and a teaspoonful or so of cold water, with a few drops vanilla essence, and knead to a firm dough. Turn on to a floured board, roll ¼ in. thick, and stamp into rounds or fancy shapes. Bake in a slow oven (350° F.) until firm and somewhat browned (about 20 minutes). Cool thoroughly before putting in a tin.

● The picture on page 31 shows how you can decorate the Christmas cake, using only 4 oz. granulated sugar, a few silver balls and about 2 yards of Cellophane ribbon. To make the icing,

Put it in the bank, it'll help to buy a tank.

TEA :
Anchovy Toas tor
Savoury Sandwiches
Biscuits
Christmas Cake
Tea (China or Indian)

dissolve the sugar in ½ gill water and bring to the boil. While it is boiling remove any scum that rises, and keep the sides of the pan free of crystals, using a brush dipped in cold water. When the temperature of 229° F. is reached, pour the syrup into a clean basin and beat until it thickens and becomes opaque, then pour on to the cake and place any decorations in position. Do not ice the cake more than one day in advance, or the icing will become discoloured.

● Prepare the custard for the trifle or fruit fool, and make the mock cream to serve with it.

Mock Whipped Cream

½ pint milk
2 teaspoonfuls corn-flour
1½ oz. unsalted margarine
3 teaspoonfuls sugar
A few drops vanilla essence

Mix the cornflour to a paste with a little of the milk, heat the rest of the milk and when boiling pour on to the blended cornflour, stirring well. Return to the saucepan, bring to the boil, and cook for 2 or 3 minutes, stirring continuously, then allow to get quite cold (it should set like a blancmange). Meanwhile cream the margarine and sugar together until *very* light and creamy. Whisk in the blancmange mixture, a little at a time, beating with a wire whisk. Lastly add vanilla.

● Prepare the Christmas Platter dish as far as possible. This is made with the following collection of cooked garden vegetables, cold meats, and fish, set out on a large dish like a giant hors d'œuvre:

Christmas Platter

1 small cauliflower
1 small white-heart cabbage
A heart of celery
A little grated onion
Salt and pepper
A variety of cooked sausages and smoked and pickled fish
Watercress
A few cooked carrots
Mock mayonnaise sauce

Cook the cauliflower (and carrot, if necessary) and allow to cool. Shred the crisp raw cabbage and celery very finely, mix them together with a little finely grated onion, and bind with mock mayonnaise sauce, adding salt and pepper to taste.

To dish, place the cauliflower in the centre of a large platter and coat it with the mock mayonnaise sauce. Arrange the slices of cooked sausage or canned meat down one side of the dish, and filleted tunny fish,

smoked herring or other piquant fish on the opposite side. Pile the cabbage and celery mixture in heaps at each end of the dish, with strips of carrot and sprigs of watercress in between.

ON CHRISTMAS DAY . . . .

● **The Bird.** Allow a young chicken about 1 hour to roast, a duck about 1¼ hours, and a goose about 1½ hours. Turkeys up to 14 lb. (weight after dressing) require 15 minutes per lb. and 15 minutes extra; allow rather less if larger. Steam a boiling fowl 2½ to 3 hours, then roast for ¼ hour.

The Gravy. Use the giblet stock for this, and make plenty, as it comes in useful when cooking up the remains of the meat.

The Potatoes. Roast these with the bird, allowing them 1 hour.

The Sprouts. Cook in a little boiling salted water for about 20 minutes. Take care not to overcook them.

The Pudding. Steam or boil 3 to 4 hours, and serve with good white sauce made with ¾ oz. each of margarine and flour and ½ pint milk, flavoured with vanilla or almond essence, and sweetened to taste.

THE DAYS AFTER . . . .

● You will want to make the remains of your bird go as far as possible. One way is to use a little of the meat in **stuffed pancakes.** Mince the meat, and any left-over vegetables, season well, and bind with gravy or a sauce. Fry some small, thin pancakes (a prepared batter mixture is suitable for these) and fill with the hot meat mixture. Serve with a green vegetable and the rest of the gravy.

A plate pie is another good dish with cooked meat. Make the mixture as above, adding a little grated onion, if possible, and bind with gravy or sauce. Line a tin plate with short-crust pastry, fill with the mixture, and cover with a pastry lid. Bake in a hot oven (450° F.) till the pastry is well browned. Serve hot or cold.

Keep some of the neater pieces of cold bird for a nourishing **salad** with all manner of winter vegetables. Cut the pieces of meat into neat strips and marinade them in a mixture of two parts salad oil to one part vinegar, with salt, pepper, mustard and chopped herbs. Mix together some diced cooked root vegetables (carrot, turnip, beetroot) and place in a salad bowl. Arrange a ring of cooked sliced

potato round the edge of the bowl, place the meat and marinade in the centre, and garnish with bunches of watercress or winter endive.

● Collect all the bones, of course, and the carcase of the bird, and add them, together with a bouquet garni, a bay leaf and a few bacon rinds, to the remainder of the giblet stock and boil gently for several hours. This gives an excellent stock, which makes many delicious soups.

Gravy Soup. Thicken the stock and season well, adding a few drops of vinegar or piquant sauce. Colour a good rich brown with gravy browning, and serve with croûtons of bread, fried or toasted.

Broth. Add diced or shredded vegetables to the stock and a little barley, season well, and simmer till tender. Add fresh chopped parsley before serving.

● **Christmas Hotch Potch.** Cut up a few carrots, a small turnip, a small swede, an onion or leek, and a few sticks of celery, and sauté them in a little dripping or bacon fat. Add half a cabbage, shredded finely, and enough of the stock just to cover. Lastly, add seasonings and a bouquet garni, and simmer until all is tender. Add more stock, if necessary, but the soup should be thick with the vegetables. Before serving remove (*Continued on page 82*)

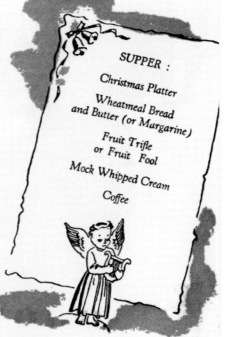

SUPPER :

Christmas Platter

Wheatmeal Bread
and Butter (or Margarine)

Fruit Trifle
or Fruit Fool

Mock Whipped Cream

Coffee

A sailor's blood is on your head if you waste a scrap of bread.

1941 was

OPEN your history books at the beginning of this new year of 1942, the third New Year of this, the second German War. Look at the little space into which the earlier wars are compressed, although each was probably bigger than its predecessor, and see how few names there are that are prominent. For the first German War you will find among others Asquith, Lloyd George, Haig, Foch and Clemenceau; Beatty and Jellicoe will be there; but, all in all, probably not more than a dozen or so have survived the last quarter of a century. And then sit down and make out your own list for 1941 and see how far it agrees with mine. I cannot in the space of one article hope to single out many of those who I think deserve to be remembered, but here are some of the names—some new, others old with a new meaning—which must be on the list. Here, too, are some names of people that most of us have already forgotten or never heard of before at all.

Starting at the top, think back to that gay summer of 1939, a summer when many of

By
ELIA

The pseudonym veils the identity of a sparkling commentator whom you've read and enjoyed, and will meet again in these pages

* Save now for a safe to-morrow.

Their Year

us basked physically in warm seas, while in our hearts we knew that at any moment the captains and the kings were going to start showing people that once again the sky was falling down. If then we talked of Winston Churchill, we would have thought of him as a rather unsuccessful politician who, always with great conviction and great courage, had looked like being leader of his country but had never quite made the grade. Now the name of Churchill is, once again, the rallying battle-cry. He is the great obvious in this names contest, the short, sturdy man who has two tremendous qualities—guts and an almost superhuman power of being able to rouse the world with his rhetoric.

Where would this country be to-day without its Churchill? Where would it be to-day if Chamberlain, Baldwin and Mac-Donald had listened to his innumerable warnings about what Germany was going to do? Besides, Churchill is essentially one of us, no matter what our trade or vocation or to what class we belong. We can all understand everything he says, and because of that we are all of us rather inclined—perhaps too inclined—to accept as right everything he does, even when we cannot understand it. His chief fault, to most of us, is that he is perhaps too loyal to his own colleagues, too resentful of criticism of them or their policies. Lloyd George, some of you will remember, had the same dynamic qualities of leadership as Churchill; but Lloyd George had a stronger team behind him, a Bonar Law to run the war machine and a Northcliffe as his great propagandist and critic when it was necessary.

On the political screen, too, are other new-old faces, the little grinning Canadian, Beaverbrook, being perhaps the chief among them; Beaverbrook with his flair for showmanship and picking men, his quick judgment and his rasping tongue. Some people call him an opportunist, principally because he is always open to conviction because he will change his views if the arguments against them are strong enough. He is a dynamo of energy, a great little engine, and, when he gets up steam, nothing will stop him till he reaches his terminus.

Of the new men who run the war there are four who I think should have mention—Lord Woolton, Bob Hudson, Lord Leathers and Ernest Bevin. Woolton, the suave shopkeeper with a wheedling voice, is too well known to the readers of GOOD HOUSEKEEPING and to radio audiences to need any comment from me. But I think he has done a good job, as good a job as the necessarily enormous size of his department will let him. Bob Hudson, our Minister of Agriculture, tall, young for a man of his eminence, rather good-looking and a fair speaker—he halts and hesitates a bit too much—has managed to make two ears of corn grow in this country where only one grew before; he has a fairly small Ministry, yet I believe it has accomplished prodigies. Agriculture in this country is back on the map again as a vital leading industry. Hudson's work will really start after the war, when he tries to keep agriculture on the heights to which he has succeeded in raising it. He has definite plans for this, and, being Hudson, he will certainly fight to the last round to get them through. Then there is Lord Leathers, almost unknown before the war outside of shipping circles. His is the job of seeing that food and munitions reach this country and are safely transported through it. He is unobtrusive, quiet and unassuming, but he looks like doing a big job well.

Ernest Bevin deserves both praise and blame, praise for his courage in taking the job as Minister of Labour, blame because he does not seem to many of us to have yet gone far enough. He has willingly put his country's good before his own, for all his life he has been the buffer between employed and employer. Now he is pulling women into war (Continued on page 42)

* They also serve who save their waste.

Background

LORD ELTON writes especi
an article worth far more
ticularly if you have

NOWADAYS most of our personal problems are coloured by the vast crisis in whose grip we live; one can hardly so much as plant the herbaceous border without taking into consideration the prospects of the war. And naturally the problem of how to ensure that one's children grow up with at least an opportunity of becoming Christians—always one of the most intimate and exacting that a parent has to face—seems to take on an added urgency in time of war.

We are locked, after all, in a death struggle with a country in which a fanatical and largely pagan faith inspires some, and is imposed upon all. Without having subscribed to it, no German citizen can hold the meanest public office. In sharp contrast, in our own country to-day hardly anyone, except the clergy, *need* be a Christian. Any parent who pleases may withdraw his child from religious instruction in the state schools. Any young man who so chooses can pass through even the ancient, residential Universities, all of them originally religious foundations, without coming into any sort of contact with any religious organisation whatever.

I do not mention these obvious facts in order to suggest that it is our business to revive religious education as part of the effort to defeat Germany—although I do, as a matter of fact, believe both that, however many tanks and aeroplanes we possess, we cannot expect to survive this war unless we are intellectually, morally and spiritually worthy to shape, as victors, the pattern of a new world era; and also that we are unlikely to be worthy to shape a new civilisation if we have lost the faith which moulded our own. My reason for recalling these familiar circumstances is partly that they do, after all, make up the setting in which our children have to get what religious education we allow them, but chiefly that they serve to suggest the heavy responsibility which rests on parents nowadays.

Whether we realise it or not, the decision as to whether our children are to grow up Christians or pagans is very much more ours than anybody else's. It is not of course entirely ours: the educational system may be too much for us. A youth whose school and college have left him spiritually as uninstructed as the beasts that perish may find himself unconsciously contrasting the science or philosophy which he has learnt at an adult level, with religion as taught at his mother's knee; he may become a

sceptic or a pagan without a notion that to be intellectually entitled to reject the Christian philosophy means not merely outgrowing *The Peep of Day* or seeing through what he remembers of the vicar's sermons, but satisfactorily disposing of St. Paul and St. Augustine, Pascal and Newman, Kierkegaard and von Hügel—a very different proposition altogether.

More often, however, it is the other way, and the home obliterates the sound influence of the school. The public schools, in particular, which are almost the last institutions in which attendance at religious worship is compulsory, often inspire a boy, or girl, in adolescence, with a secret idealism, and with speculations as to that which lies beyond the veil of the material world. These are frail and sensitive growths, speedily extinguished in the child who goes back in the holidays to a home which revolves round the bridge table or the golf course, and parents who obviously regard religion as just another school "subject," the concern of clergymen and schoolmasters, to be comfortably shelved, with algebra or Latin, out of school hours.

NINE children out of ten, perhaps indeed all children, if they are given a reasonable opportunity, or rather if no special obstacles are put in their way, will take naturally to religion—children after all were suggested by the best of all authorities as a model for those who wished to find their way into the Kingdom of Heaven. All ought therefore to be particularly easy. And yet, perplexingly, it isn't. A couple of generations ago, before church-going and Bible-reading had ceased to be national habits, it was doubtless all much easier. Many of a parent's problems were solved then by the conventions. To-day he has to solve them for himself. It is easy enough, no doubt, if the household contains a saint—as it surprisingly often does. A devout and selfless mother will teach her family more about religion, without knowing it, than a hundred Bible lessons. But if there are no saints?

THE problem is shelved, but not solved, by parents who take the line of least resistance, saying to their children, in effect, "We shall not dictate your opinions. As far as we are concerned, you are free to believe anything, or nothing." Here, too, neutrality is impossible. The experi-

Munitions are no good in the home—turn out that waste paper.

for Living

ally for Good Housekeeping
than casual reading—par-
children of your own

ence of the ages means one thing, or the other. The scientist will probably encourage his pupil to take Sir Isaac Newton's conclusions for granted; conceivably he may tell him to reject them, but he certainly will not say that it is a matter of indifference whether they are accepted or not.

MOST children are taught some simple prayers in infancy. That is fairly plain sailing. Usually, I suspect, they continue to say their nursery prayers long after they have become a meaningless formula, and they themselves are old enough for something more enterprising; I seem to remember that at my preparatory school my own efforts consisted of my nursery formula plus a few very topical personal petitions—as that I might not bowl full pitches to leg in the school match to-morrow. At that comparatively early stage in a boy's career parents, I imagine, usually disclaim further responsibility for that part of his religious education. At any rate he has been taught to say some prayers; what precisely he says is henceforth his own look out—unless and until the pastor or master who prepares him for confirmation chooses to look into the matter. I cannot help suspecting that, before disclaiming further responsibility, one ought to have contrived to convey the idea that prayer means something more than asking for favours.

ONE of the most familiar problems comes very early. Ought one to compel children to go to church—however much they grumble? Personally, I believe that one should. I know all the arguments the other way. What good can it do to go in a rebellious mood? Children will get enough compulsory

church-going at school. Church-going should not be a parade.

The arguments leave me unmoved. One has to form plenty of useful habits unwillingly, when one is a child, from having to brush one's teeth, upwards. And it has always seemed to me that there are conclusive reasons for taking children to church, whatever their own inclinations may be. For one thing, a church, particularly an old church, is a *good* place, full of (Continued on page 40)

Illustrations by Jack Matthew

— JACK MATTHEW —

* *If every home gave a book a week, it would make 240,000 tons of waste paper a year.*

"*For* THOSE *in* PERIL *on the* SEA"

"WE have always been the Cinderella of the Services, but now at last we seem to have found fairy god-mothers!" So wrote the Master of a merchant vessel to a knitting party who had provided comforts for his crew.

We are all proud of our seafaring traditions, proud that the Dunkirk armada was manned by Tom, Dick and Harry, fisherman, ferryman, amateur yachtsman. Perhaps it is because we are so used to this tradition that we have taken it too much for granted, and have paid less attention than we should to the men who maintain it. At any rate, when war broke out, and welfare schemes of all sorts were started for sailors, soldiers, airmen, factory workers, many people seemed to assume that merchant seamen could carry on their dangerous job without any extra attention.

There were several societies, notably the British Ship Adoption Society, which did their best to provide comforts for the sailors, but it was not until 1940 that the Merchant Navy Comforts Service was formally registered, and began its great work on behalf of the seamen.

Behind it were the shipowners—notably the owner of a fleet of cargo vessels Mr. Edmund Watts, and the Officers' and Men's organisations of the Merchant Navy, who knew better than most of us how greatly the perils of seafaring had been increased by war.

One of the worst things was the plight of torpedoed sailors. Those who were lucky enough to be picked up by destroyers arrived on board with everything lost, frequently half-frozen, with their clothes in rags. They had to depend on the kindness of naval ratings for any odd garments they could get, and newspapers often published pictures of these survivors coming ashore scantily wrapped in blankets.

THIS problem the Comforts Service set itself to tackle, and in the summer of 1941 it launched a big-scale appeal for Emergency Rescue Kits. The scheme was simple: the Admiralty had agreed to pack aboard destroyers and escort ships sacks containing a complete outfit of clothes, which would be handed out to torpedoed seamen when they came aboard. The clothes were a gift, and would provide for the men not merely on board, but during the time while they waited for grants and coupons to replace what they had lost.

So the Society launched its appeal from the Appeal Headquarters in Hampstead, and I heard something about the response from the man who directed the campaign, Mr. Kirkland Bridge. He is a person who really does merit that ill-used adjective "dynamic." A young middle-aged man, with horn-rimmed glasses, a square chin and a brisk, confident way of talking, you have only got to spend a few moments with him to realise that he is bubbling over

After days in an open boat, our seamen bless the Merchant Navy Comforts Service

with ideas and enterprise.

"Between June and December, 1941," he told me, "we raised £112,000, including £11,000 from a wireless appeal made by Mr. Edmund Watts. In fact, we did so well that at the moment we just don't want any more money for this particular cause—though there are plenty of other things for which we *do* need money and help."

With commendable imagination, the sponsors of the appeal made use of a human touch which pleased both those who gave and the men who received. Every person or group of people who provided the £2 necessary to supply an outfit was sent a label, colourfully printed in the national red, white and blue. On this they wrote their names and addresses, and, if they wanted, a personal message of goodwill to the unknown seamen who would eventually wear the clothes. This label was wrapped in the handkerchief which, tucked into the trouser pocket,

Rubber salvage is vital NOW.

"*As Poles, these gifts touch our hearts profoundly, coming from your British homes. We are proud and glad to be serving together with your great and noble nation*"

"*We were five days in an open boat, and on rescue were made very comfortable on board one of H.M. ships, the officers and ratings being most kind. Unhappily we were unable to take much with us, and the warm comforts so kindly given by the Merchant Navy Comforts Service were invaluable in the cold Atlantic weather*"

"*Our duties at present lie in a particularly bleak part of the world, and you may imagine how gratefully gifts have been received by all hands*"

Above are some typical letters of thanks

them, and have formed Merchant Navy knitting parties to help.

After seeing Mr. Bridge, I went down to Essex, where the headquarters of the Society have been evacuated to a solid Victorian country house, Canfield Moat, near Great Dunmow. They used to be in the City of London, in the midst of the shipping world, but when the blitz started it was decided to safeguard the valuable stocks of comforts by moving them out of London.

The person in charge here is Mrs. Margaret Watts, wife of the shipowner. She is only thirty, dark, slim, smart, incredibly competent. With the assistant secretary, Mrs. Maryon-Wilson, who used to run a wool shop, and knows everything there is to be known about knitting, with a nucleus of paid staff, and a splendid body of voluntary workers, all (Continued on page 47)

completed the outfit. The effectiveness of this brainwave is obvious. It means a lot to people to know that their gifts will remain personal, instead of being swallowed up in a communal pool. It also —as the letters of thanks received by the hundred testify—meant a good deal to the sailors to realise that individuals all over the country were interested in their welfare.

"Now that the rescue kit scheme is fairly launched," said Mr. Bridge, "we are concentrating on our Standard Sacks. Merchant seamen don't wear uniforms, and often their own clothes are unsuitable for the climate and duration of wartime voyages. So we send them sacks of comforts, sweaters, socks, scarves, gloves, helmets, and so on, with enough in each sack for five men."

Unlike the suits and underclothes of the rescue kits, which were bought with the money contributed, these comforts are almost entirely provided by people who have volunteered to knit

WAR in the GARDEN

By George E. Whitehead, F.R.H.S.

" Deep in a silent chamber of the rose
There was a fattened worm. He looked
around,
Espied a relative and spoke at him :
' It seems to me this world is very good.' "

APRIL is here and everything seems to know it. The birds, animals, insects, trees, flowers, grass and weeds are exuberant, while human beings are shedding their winter "clobber" and looking around for an outlet for fresh endeavours. If we pause to think about this we are apt to become sanguine or desperate, according to our temperaments. To me, it is all wonderful, this rebirth of Nature, especially when the particular subjects do no harm to anything else. Unfortunately, gardening is "not all roses," in fact, there would be no roses at all if the dreadful maggots were allowed to ravage unchecked, and it is our unthankful task to eliminate the aggressors. As these aggressions often begin in April, we must make up our minds to put our feet down, or use syringes or hatpins, or whatever weapons are most efficacious.

Slugs prowl in damp, warm weather. Young delphiniums and lettuces are their favourite foods, although they will be content with anything else within reach. If it can be obtained, the best eliminator is Meta. A packet can be obtained from a chemist at small cost. To use, crush one tablet into powder and mix it with a pint of bran (obtained from the baker) and lay that about in small heaps among the attacked plants. If no Meta is obtainable, try to get a proprietary slug - killer from a seedsman, as it will probably contain the same chemical. Another alternative is to place little heaps of bran about and put slates or boards over them. If lifted daily, the chances are that some slugs will be lurking in the bran all ready to be collected and destroyed. I know a lady who takes a vicious delight in stabbing them with a hatpin and dropping them into a can of brine. I use my fingers, but recommend squeamish people to lift the slugs with a pair of old sugar-tongs.

Incidentally, slugs' eggs can often be found in clusters, looking like largish translucent pills. Gather these up proficiently and burn them.

Wireworms are as bad as U-boats. We cannot see them torturing the vegetable roots, neither can we do a lot to stop them, beyond setting traps and patiently clearing these daily. Pieces of carrots or potatoes buried just under the surface of the bed will lure the worms into capture. If you stick skewers in the pieces of roots, toffee-apple fashion, before burying them you will know where they are and be able to pull them up comfortably. Wireworms are also attracted to old bones and, if of no use for salvage, these are excellent additional traps when planted a few inches deep. By the way, a wireworm is about an inch long, is evenly thin, and looks as if it has been varnished.

Birds are a nuisance upon seed beds, but they are not pests and should only be looked upon as naughty children that must be checked. Strands of cotton criss-crossed upon sticks about nine inches above ground level will frighten them. If cotton is not easily got, two pieces of window-pane suspended upon an arched stake will keep them away for several days. These should be hung up with two pieces of string that are tied close together so that the dangling bits of glass jingle together as they sway in the breeze, and at the same time throw rays when the sun shines.

Greenflies are sure to be about in April. There are about three hundred different kinds of these, and they all breed at an alarming rate. Happily for us, they can be eliminated without much effort. Whenever I see them upon the roses or carnations or any other plants, I mix up a bucket of quassia extract (obtained from the sundriesman) according to instructions, drop the suction end of a Solo sprayer in the mixture, and behave as though the greenflies were a fire and my appliance a stirrup pump. A makeshift wash can be made by dissolving a bar of *(Continued on page 50)*

APRIL REMINDERS

● *Sow maincrop carrots about the middle of month, the best varieties being those with Intermediate in the name. Space rows 1 ft. apart, sow thinly and shallowly.*

● *Sow mid-season peas twice during the month, suitable varieties being Onward, Senator and Telephone. Space rows as far apart as the peas grow high, e.g. 3-ft. high peas need 3-ft. rows and so forth. Spinach, or spinach substitutes such as Swiss Chards, or turnips may be sown between tall rows.*

● *May is the month to sow maincrop beet, but an early Globe variety may be sown now if this vegetable is a favourite. Space rows 15 in. asunder and make drills an inch deep.*

● *It is not too late to sow onions and parsnips, but do not delay another day.*

● *In a nursery bed, sow a row each of winter broccoli—varieties named Adam's Early, Knight's Protecting and Snow's Winter White. In the same bed sow cabbage, early savoy and late cauliflower, the best variety of each being Autumn Drumhead, Dwarf Green Curled and Veitch's Autumn Giant respectively. Also sow Cos lettuce Giant White, cabbage lettuce Matchless and parsley Perfection Moss Curled. Space all rows 1 ft. apart and transplant the seedlings when large enough.*

● *Plant maincrop potatoes at every opportunity, spacing rows 2 ft. apart at least, and tubers within the rows half that distance.*

● *April is the best month in which to dress paths with weedkiller.*

* Salvage is a National Service.

Drawings by C. F. Tunnicliffe

I REGISTERED ON SATURDAY

What do all these women and girls think as they line up in the Employment Exchanges to register for National Service? In this article a Scots-woman speaks for many of her contemporaries

BY JANETTA M. McDONALD

ONE Saturday, not so very long ago, I presented myself at the Labour Exchange between the hours of four and five p.m., and had "my particulars" taken. We were a curious assortment: young mothers with two or three children stood next to typists, domestic servants, doctors, teachers and what-not. Twenty-five years ago we had entered a world at war. Now we were being called upon to fight in this new struggle.

Many things had happened in those twenty-five years. Yet, at the time, how little difference they had made to the lives of most of us. Being women, we had not bothered very much about what was happening around us. Other people, we thought, may be to blame for this war, but *we've* had no hand in the events which have landed us here in the Labour Exchange. We are willing to do what we can, now that the war is here. But please understand, everybody, you can't blame us for what has happened—we've had nothing to do with it.

And that, perhaps, is the point. We've had nothing to do with it. What, then, have we to do with war? Well, obviously, we've got to have something to do with it, whether we like it or not. We can't avoid it. We've got to help to defend ourselves and our country from attack. Of course, there's more in it than that. In fighting for ourselves we're fighting for the liberties of a subject Europe. We're fighting for the chance to try to make a worth-while world out of the mess that has been handed over to us. We can't dodge our responsibilities now, however much we may have done so in the past.

Have we done so in the past? Well, let's see what we have allowed to happen since we became capable of thinking for ourselves.

We were only fifteen when the first major post-last-war aggression took place. At that age, perhaps, we could be excused for not paying very much attention to Japan's invasion of Manchuria in 1931.

When Italy attacked Abyssinia in 1935 some of us were a little disturbed by the tales we heard of the Italians attacking the helpless Abyssinians with poison gas and bomber. And hadn't the League of Nations professed to put an end to such aggressions? Still, at nineteen, we weren't very interested in events in far-off Africa.

War came nearer home in 1936 when the Fascist revolt started in Spain. Non-intervention was in the air, and on the face of it, it seemed quite reasonable. Let the Spaniards fight it out for themselves! One couldn't believe all the stories one heard of German and Italian aeroplanes, tanks and men fighting on the side of the rebels. Why should *we* interfere? We didn't pretend to understand about Spain—it was all so confused.

A year later Japan's attack on China jolted us a little. But then the war jogged on, and we soon learned to skip the descriptions of the latest Japanese bombing escapades, and to view the numbed masses of Chinese refugees in the news-reel with unconcern. That is, we were sorry for them, but the Japs were responsible for that misery, not us.

Everywhere, human beings were suffering. In Germany people were dismissed from their employment, imprisoned and tortured because of their race, religion or political opinions. Such misery could not be confined within the walls of a prison, even though that prison were a whole country. We heard of it here in Britain. But how could we believe that such things were happening in the twentieth century? Such stories were always greatly exaggerated.

Of the self-subjection of the German people to thraldom, we could make nothing. We had no time to find out the causes which led them to adopt Adolf Hitler as their saviour, or even to try to understand why they should feel themselves in need of a saviour. But their misery, too, must have been great.

Perhaps it was because things were everywhere so terrible, that the protective armour of indifference hardened around our brain and emotions. To feel the misery of all the peoples of the world, in those twenty-five years, would be to make living itself intolerable.

Events moved swiftly; Austria was annexed without a murmur.

Suddenly, in September 1938, we shrank back aghast from the spreading waves of the world's misery. But the Peace of Munich restored our natural optimism. Hitler had got the people and defences of Czechoslovakia, but we still had our Peace. We still had so many other things to think about, we all had our own interests. Some of us were studying for degrees, some of us were working hard to make a success of our jobs. Others of us were living in the romantic world of the engaged or newly-married. What if at times we had an uneasy suspicion that things were not what they should be

Don't forget your shopping basket!

A Smart Woman's Choice—

Drawings by Tage Werner

Saved scraps decide the issue of the big scrap.

Individually made Clothes

By

The Clothes

Consultant

IT'S smart, in more senses than one, to make your own clothes, for, with the guidance of a good pattern, you can dress yourself with distinction, and yet save very appreciably. This month I have chosen two patterns that are straightforward and simple to follow, and have the additional merit of being very adaptable.

On the left-hand page we present that invaluable summer standby, the redingote. It makes up equally well in a fine wool or a heavy rayon, doesn't date and looks equally "well-dressed" in town and country. Though designed primarily as a coat, this pattern makes a grand coat-dress, too. Cut out and sew exactly as instructions, but wear over an existing slip which has full-length front panel of material to match or tone with the redingote. If preferred, have the panel (better still, two different-coloured panels) separate, and press stud into the front of the redingote.

In the picture, the lady sitting down has made up her coat-dress in a print and added crisp white sharkskin revers, made from pattern 1375. This pattern is particularly useful, as it gives details for making ten different kinds of "lingerie touches" (of which we illustrate three), including a well-cut waistcoat front.

Smart though a white accent looks, it is by no means necessary with this redingote dress. To break the severity of the neckline you can add a shaggy chrysanthemum made of odd scraps of the material, or simply wear a triple row of beads, or one of the little necklaces made of shells, or flowers, that are now so popular.

Do try the three-quarter sleeves; they are so smart this season, and also so adaptable. However, if you prefer them, the design does include instructions for an ordinary coat sleeve, as you will see from the little back view; the choice is yours.

The right-hand page sketch shows a dress that will prove the answer to your prayer if you have got two short lengths of material to make up, for skirt and sleeves are in one colour, and the slick blouse-top in another. This design makes up particularly well with printed top and solid-coloured skirt and sleeves, though in a light and darker plain material, or all in one colour, it is equally effective. The line of the yoke is new, and the skirt has just the right amount of fullness to be generally becoming. Our thumb-nail sketches suggest two methods of trimming (on a one-colour dress) that are much favoured by the better designers to-day. The first is a soft cotton cord, or rope, in a contrasting colour. The other, a flat "peasanty" looking braid embroidery in two or more tones to contrast. A suggestion you might like to follow is to have a turban, or a peasant scarf, trimmed to match the dress.

Butterick pattern 1853. *Redingote in wool or rayon; bust size* 38 *in. takes* 2½ *yards* 54-*in., or* 2⅝ *yards if full-length sleeves are required. In* 35-*rayon, it takes* 4 *yards with long sleeves, and slightly less with three-quarter ones. Bust sizes* 30-48 *in. Price* 2s. 9d., *plus* 6d. *purchase tax.*

Butterick pattern 1375. *Lingerie accessories, including collars, cuffs and waistcoat, made in three sizes. Price* 1s. 3d., *plus* 3d. *purchase tax.*

Butterick pattern 1849. "*Quick-and-easy*" *dress pattern. Size* 34-*in. bust takes* 1½ *yards of* 35-*in. material for the blouse top and* 2⅝ *yards for the skirt and sleeves. All one colour, it takes* 2½ *yards of* 54-*in. fabric. Made in bust sizes* 30-44 *in. Price* 2s. 9d., *plus* 6d. *purchase tax.*

Now *that* Soap *is* Rationed

By
P. L. GARBUTT

**Director of Good
Housekeeping Institute**

*This is the soap allowance for a family of four, apportioned equally
between soap flakes, laundry soap, No. 1 soap powder, and toilet soap*

Small wonder that there are always laundry problems in the Institute mail, now
that soap is rationed and laundries often will not accept new customers. It is not easy
to make the soap last out, especially where there are children, but you can help yourself quite a lot by taking a little trouble.

Here are some of the questions we have been asked recently, and among them
may be your problem, too. If not, write and let us know your difficulty.

Query I : Soap Rationing

The first question comes from the
mother of a family who is anxious to
know how she can best soften water
and so save her soap ration. This
question is published because it is a
difficulty shared to some extent by all
readers just now.

Our Advice

(1) Install a mains softener if, like
our questioner, you live in a hard-
water district, are able to secure a
model, and can meet the cost. (We
ascertained, by the way, that models
were available at the time of writing.)

(2) Alternatively, collect and use
rain-water for washing and household
cleaning purposes, if possible.

(3) If, for one reason or another, the
above suggestions are impracticable,
use soda to soften the water, but be
very careful not to use too much,
especially when washing delicate articles. Actually, *very little* indeed is
required, far less than most people
imagine.

The simplest and safest way of using
washing soda is to dissolve 1 oz. in a
pint of water and bottle this solution,
adding about 1 tablespoonful to every
gallon of hot water for every 5 degrees
of hardness, i.e., for water of 20 degrees
of hardness, add 4 tablespoonfuls per
gallon. (Your water company will tell

you the degree of hardness of your water
supply.) Place requisite quantity of soda
solution in a bowl before running in
the hot water, and leave for a moment or
two, if possible, so that it has a chance
of reacting with the hardness before
you add the soap. This may sound a
little complicated, but is actually very
simple once you have ascertained the
hardness of your water and measured
up the bowl or bath you generally use.
Adding the required amount of soda
before the soap will, indeed, soon become a habit, and a very worthwhile
one, which may save you a really big
proportion of your soap ration, possibly as much as a quarter.

Query II : Washing Woollens

"After using lukewarm water for
years, I have been told that woollens
can be washed successfully with boiling water. I should like to have your
opinion."

Our Advice

We explained to our reader that
there are several satisfactory ways of
washing woollens, and that one involves the use of practically boiling
water. This method gives very good
results, provided care is taken not
to immerse the wool in cold water immediately after the hot. If, however,

articles are left in the washing water
until cool enough to handle, and rinsing water of about the same temperature is used, no harm will result.
Many people prefer to wash woollens
in this way rather than in the more
usually accepted one, involving the use
of water at about blood heat.

Things to avoid when washing woollens are: (1) rubbing, which very soon
causes felting and shrinkage; (2) ex-
tremes of temperature; (3) the use of
strong alkalies, such as soda, all of
which are injurious.

Query III : Substitutes for Laundry Starch

"Can you tell me of any satisfactory
substitute for laundry starch, which is
now unprocurable in my district?"

Our Advice

We explained that satisfactory substitutes for laundry starch are farina-
ceous substances, such as flour, rice-
water, etc., all of which are valuable
foodstuffs and should, therefore, not
be used for other than feeding purposes in war-time. For thin muslin
articles gum arabic is sometimes used,
but this only gives very slight stiffen-
ing, and may not be easy to obtain at
the present time. In any case, it is
unsuitable for heavy articles.

* *Keep a daily check on your dustbin.*

The Dawn of a New Age — Plastics

By a Market Research Expert

IT seems incredible that any material benefits can be derived from the immense destructive forces of modern warfare, yet in the past war has proved to be the greatest stimulus to progress in our industrial development. After all, the desire to survive is the strongest force in life, and just as men and women are spurred on by danger to the peak of mental and physical effort, so, too, does industry exert every effort to produce the necessary weapons.

Urgency and the strange merchandise of war introduce new materials, new machinery and swifter methods of production than hitherto achieved, and inventive genius is accorded a recognition which would be impossible in the more conservative times of peace. So when the " sound and the fury " of battle have died away, we shall have reached a stage of progress in the manufacturing field which many of us might never have seen in our lifetime, had normal conditions prevailed without the interruption of war. When the vast and efficient machinery which for so long has produced only weapons of destruction is adapted to manufacture the domestic requirements of peace, we may look forward to revolutionary changes in our surroundings and standards of living. New products will embody all the improvements in material, design and large-scale production gained as a result of these difficult times.

Remember that until the outbreak of war in 1914 flying was not taken seriously by the majority of people, but its possibilities as a weapon forced us to concentrate upon the development and production of aircraft, resulting in progress which would have been impossible in a similar period of peace (though in those days they were not the armoured giants we now see in the skies, but wood and fabric structures requiring special treatment to withstand the elements).

With the development of aircraft came the enormous demand for celluloid, a demand that created a vast new industry which eventually had to find a peace-time outlet and resulted in Rayon. Thus artificial silk became available to everyone and set a new standard in clothing and furnishing—no longer were silken hose, underwear and dresses the prerogative of the wealthy.

The 1914–18 war also revealed our shortcomings in the production of dyes, optical and scientific instruments, etc., for the supply of which we had largely

ONE new type of plastic makes this unbreakable, porcelain-finished beaker (by British Industrial Plastics, Ltd.), now installed in every lifeboat, while at the other end of the scale, plastics are already being used for aeroplane and motor-car bodies

depended upon Germany. New factories were built and labour was trained to meet the urgent requirements, and with the passing of war these huge industrial plants turned their resources to civilian needs. Thus in 1913, the year before the last war, the imports of hollow-ware (saucepans, kettles, etc.) into this country were 13,500 tons. This represented four out of every six hollow-ware articles we then required. But the factories which produced weapons during the war afterwards turned to making domestic utensils, and in 1938 we were importing less than one out of every six such articles.

This war has again compelled us to review our requirements and marshal our resources to meet them, and intensive research is opening up many new discoveries.

It is certain that any new or improved materials which, after the drab years of war, will enrich and beautify our surroundings, and at the same time ensure the swiftest method of satisfying what will undoubtedly be an unprecedented demand, will be gratefully seized upon. There are such materials—Plastics—and it is in this industry that the greatest progress has been made during recent years.

Plastics, as we have known them up to now, are in their infancy, but important developments have been taking place, of necessity mainly confined to war production for the time being, and materials are being produced which will astonish and delight us when they become available for domestic uses.

You will be wise to reject any impression that plastics are an inferior substitute for other materials ; they have beauty and individual qualities of their own unobtainable in other materials.

Any new material that is put into general use is, in a sense, a substitute, inasmuch as it takes the place of something else. But the change is usually a progressive one. When iron and steel replaced wood for many purposes, they were substitutes, but nobody would say, in the light of present-day knowledge, that these materials were inferior substitutes for shipbuilding, bridges and similar engineering wonders.

Neither are plastics all alike. When we speak of " metal," we mean a great variety of materials with different properties. There are hard metals such as steel ; soft metals like tin ; brittle metals like cast-iron ; pliable metals like copper ; heavy metals like

* The smallest scrap YOU rescue may mean the turning point of war.

Boarding-House BLUES

—and how to cure them

MARY GRAY

goes to the heart of a

problem at present

troubling more

than a few women,

especially the

older ones

I WAS very surprised the other day to hear from an old family friend, Mrs. Alcott, whom I have known since a child. Since the war I'd lost touch with her. She said, "I do wish you could manage to come and see me —I should love to talk over old times. You see, since I've been bombed out of my home I've been living in this small, private hotel, and I'm so lonely with all my friends scattered."

So I went. The hotel is a pretty place and the garden runs down to the river. There are pleasant rooms in which to sit, but oh! what a lot of women were sitting!

When we went out for a stroll I said to Mrs. Alcott, "Are those women there all the time, just sitting doing nothing?"

"Yes," she said, "most of them are in the same circumstances as I am. It *is* bad luck, isn't it? We aren't young any more, and it's hard to be robbed of our homes, and in some cases separated from our husbands, at our time of life."

"Were they all bombed out?" I asked in surprise.

"Oh, not all," she told me. "Others have had to leave home because their husbands changed their jobs, or their families went away."

"What a pity they don't try to do something," I said. "They'd be much happier."

"I suppose you're getting in a little dig at me, too," she smiled, "but what can we do? You younger people never really understand what it means to grow old."

I said, "I'm not so young that I can't understand or appreciate what age could do, left to its own devices. But why leave it? After all, what is this business of being young? It's a question mainly of mental outlook, isn't it? Do you remember that saying, 'a broken spirit drieth up the bones'? It's when the spirit goes that old age takes a free hand."

She glanced at me, half puzzled, half amused, and then she said, vaguely: "But it's so difficult!"

"What is?" I asked.

"Forcing yourself to be occupied," she said, "when at bottom we feel so useless. We've had our best years, and now we're uprooted and more conscious than ever of our limitations."

"Surely the best years are simply the active years," I argued. "And those are only over when you begin living in the past and dragging through the present."

"Dragging through the present," she repeated. "Yes, that's what a lot of us are doing to-day, I'm afraid. But what else can we do when we have to live in hotels, when housework and shopping are done for us and there's simply no incentive?"

"You'd all find the incentive," I said, "if you'd scrape away the habits of your old life, forget what you've done in the past, and concentrate on what it's possible to do now. Even little odd jobs like sewing for other women at work all day, or simply dusting your own room, would help to stop idleness creeping on you to such an extent that in the end everything seems a hopeless effort, even reading a book. When that happens you really begin to break down and get physically ill as well."

"It's funny you should say that," she said. "I don't know if you noticed Mrs. Markham? She can't seem to do anything at all, not even knitting, which keeps a good many of us going. All she does is live for the week-ends when her husband comes down. I've often thought she'll make herself ill."

"And in the meantime I bet she worries her husband to death," I said, "by telling him how miserable she is."

"I'm afraid she does," said Mrs. Alcott, "and I know he thought it would be best for her in a hotel, as he was away so much. But now he's fretting because she's so unhappy and always brooding."

(Continued on page 88)

THE GOVERNMENT'S GIFT TO WOMEN—

Smart Clothes

WITH THE "UTILITY" LABEL

Difficult to get? Of course! Everything that's good is in short supply now, but persevere, go on asking for "double guarantee" * clothes, such as these sketched here, and do not be put off with unlabelled substitutes. The country's best fashion-goods manufacturers have put themselves, heart and soul, into the task of making good-looking, good-wearing, quality clothes that meet all the Government's demands for economy in material, labour and ~~labour~~ and they have succeeded handsomely!

* The guarantee of a fashion-house label plus that of the "Utility" C.C. label.

The dress, in a feather-weight navy/natural/ woollen with plain navy contrast, is styled by Hartnell and made by Berkertex. 57s. 9d. Similar styles in brown, powder blue, etc.

The suit, by Jaeger, in a firm-textured mono-tone woollen with lined jacket, price 97s. 4d.

The coat, also by Jaeger, is slickly tailored from good-quality herringbone type tweed, price 95s. 1d.

The Land

More people are employed in agriculture than in any other single British industry, and more people must now be fed by home-grown food than ever before. These two facts are ample reason for our commentator's choice of subject this month

by ELIA

"IF you want my monument, look around you''; these words in Latin, the epitaph of Sir Christopher Wren, architect of many famous London buildings, are in St. Paul's Cathedral, his chief work. I am going to apply them not to the towns or buildings of Britain, but to its smiling fields and pastures, to-day the living monument, not only to the thousands of farmers who earn their living from the soil, not only to the innumerable war-time farmers who have sprung up, but to the few people who are behind our great agricultural revival. And while you are reading this article, I would ask you to remember that the farmers of Britain, the stone which the builders rejected in peace-time, are to-day corner-stones of our war effort.

You might not think it, but agriculture employs more people than any other British industry (unless you class iron and steel together as one industry), and, although there are not as many people as formerly working to-day on each arable acre, this is not because fewer acres are being farmed—quite the reverse—but because the panzer divisions of farming, mechanisation, tractors and the like, are introduced on a higher scale in Britain than anywhere else in the world, including the United States.

Illustration by James and Patricia Hart

we live on

We have now—and I defy you to find these figures boring—six million more acres under the plough than we had before the war; we have now one tractor for about every three farms, and there are roughly 336,000 farms in Britain. Before the war there were 1,600,000 acres in this country under wheat; last year there were over two million. Potatoes, the most difficult crop of all to grow and harvest, because they require more man-power and more attention, have increased from 700,000 acres before the war to over a million. Green vegetables, which we used to import from the Low Countries and the Channel Islands and the rest of the world, have increased since the war by no less than one and a half million tons, quite apart from allotment crops. Finally, digest this astonishing fact: the whole of our domestic sugar ration is grown and produced in Britain. Sugar is imported, but the imports are used for other than domestic purposes.

So much for large-scale production; when I tell you that the smaller movements among individuals have resulted in 972,000 small poultry-keepers, 1,750,000 allotment holders—twice the pre-war figure—and 100,000 rabbit-keepers, you will get some idea of how much the population of this country is using its own land for its existence. Mr. Churchill himself takes the keenest interest in rabbit keepers, for it was the keeping of rabbits that saved Germany from starvation in the last war; it is hoped that the figure of 100,000 rabbit-keepers will grow to a million.

How has all this happened, who should get the credit for initiative and enterprise, who are the individuals, as yet unhonoured and unsung, who merit the country's thanks? I will tell you; but first I must give more than full marks to the County and District War Agriculture Committees, all of them voluntary workers toiling away under the direction of the Minister of Agriculture, Mr. Robert Hudson. He has, as one of his advisers, Mr. William Gavin, C.B.E., who was seconded to the Ministry of Agriculture when war broke out—a charming, quiet, likeable man who, under a rather placid, pipe-smoking exterior, conceals a depth of knowledge and a dynamic energy. Of the Minister himself—and he is a good Minister; I wish we could say the (Continued on page 48)

MANAGING WITHOUT

A good sauce will make all the difference to most steamed, and many baked and fried dishes. It used to be said of England that she had a hundred religions but only one sauce. The days of this jibe are past, we hope, even for wartime England! Excellent sauces can be made with little or no milk; here are varied recipes

FOUNDATION RECIPES

Savoury Sauce

1 oz. margarine	½ pint bone, fish or
1 oz. flour	vegetable stock (or
Flavouring ingredi-	rice, haricot bean or
ent (see below)	macaroni boilings)
Salt and pepper	

Melt the margarine and stir in the flour to form a roux. Add the liquid by degrees, then bring to the boil, stirring all the time. Cook for 1 to 2 minutes, beating the sauce with a wooden spoon to make it smooth and glossy. Season and flavour to taste.

Savoury Sauce (economical)

1 oz. flour	Knob of margarine,
½ pint liquid (as	if available
above)	Flavouring ingredi-
Salt and pepper	ent (see below)

Blend the flour to a smooth cream with a little of the liquid. Heat the remaining liquid and pour on to the blended flour, stirring. Return to the saucepan and bring to the boil, stirring all the time. Cook for 1 or 2 minutes, beating the sauce to make it smooth and glossy. Beat in a knob of margarine, if available, then season and flavour to taste.

Savoury Sauce (using potato)

1 large potato (about	1–2 teaspoonfuls
½ lb.)	chopped onion or
½ pt. water	leek
A knob of margarine	Flavouring ingredi-
Salt and pepper	ent

Melt the knob of margarine (cooking fat or dripping will do) in a saucepan and sauté the finely chopped onion in it for a few minutes, until tender. Scrub the potato and peel it thinly, then slice it into a pan, adding the water and seasoning. Cover and simmer gently until the potato disintegrates, then beat up well with a fork until smooth. Add the flavouring ingredient, re-season, if necessary, and use as required.

Note.—If you have mashed potatoes over, use these to make the sauce instead of raw potatoes. Add the mashed potatoes to the sautéd onion and stir in enough water or vegetable stock to give the desired consistency. Add seasoning and simmer a few moments before adding the flavouring.

SUGGESTIONS FOR FLAVOURING THE FOUNDATION SAUCES

1. Piquant Parsley Sauce

Add 1 to 2 tablespoonfuls freshly chopped parsley and a dash of vinegar immediately before serving. Good with fish, meat or vegetable dishes.

2. Watercress Sauce

Chop half a bunch of watercress and add it at the last moment. Good with boiled or steamed fish dishes.

3. Cheese Sauce

Add 2 to 3 oz. grated cheese and season with mustard and a few drops of piquant sauce or vinegar. Good with vegetables or fish dishes.

4. Anchovy Sauce

Add a teaspoonful or so of anchovy essence and a drop of pink colouring, omitting salt when seasoning. Good with all fish dishes.

5. Quick Curry Sauce

Add a teaspoonful of curry powder and a tablespoonful of finely chopped onion, frying them lightly in the fat when making the sauce. Good with fish or vegetable dishes.

6. Mock Hollandaise Sauce

Blend together a level tablespoonful dried egg with 1 tablespoonful malt vinegar and 1 teaspoonful tarragon vinegar. Stir this into the sauce and reheat gently, taking care not to curdle the egg. Good with fish or vegetable dishes.

The Ministry of Food

MILK

By
Jane Creswell
*Combined Domestic
Science Diploma
(Gloucester)*

Mustard Sauce

½ oz. margarine
½ oz. flour
¼ pint stock or vege-
table liquor
1–1½ teaspoonfuls
mustard

1 teaspoonful
chopped gherkin
or other pickle
1 tablespoonful vine-
gar
Salt and pepper

Melt the margarine, add the flour
and stir in the stock by degrees. Bring
to the boil and cook for two minutes,
stirring. Blend the mustard with the
vinegar and add this to the sauce.
Season well, and add a teaspoonful
finely chopped pickle, if liked.

Note.—If the sauce is to be served
with fish, fish stock may take the place
of bone stock or vegetable liquor.

Sharp Sauce (quickly made)

1 gill vegetable liquor
or stock
1 small teaspoonful
cornflour
Gravy colouring

Salt and pepper
2 teaspoonfuls
piquant sauce
2 teaspoonfuls malt
vinegar

Blend the cornflour with a little of
the liquid, heat the remainder and,
when boiling, add it, stirring. Return
to the pan and cook for 2 minutes,
stirring continuously. Then season
and colour a rich brown with gravy
colouring. Just before serving add the
piquant sauce and vinegar.

Brown Sauce

¼ oz. dripping
1 small onion or leek
A piece of carrot,
turnip and celery
½ pint vegetable
stock

Salt and pepper
½ teaspoonful vege-
table extract or
ketchup
Gravy colouring
A bunch of herbs

½ oz. flour

Melt the dripping in a saucepan, add
the chopped onion or leek and fry a
good brown colour. Add the flavouring
vegetables, cut in small pieces, or
chopped, and the stock and herbs.
Season with salt and pepper, cover and
simmer gently for half an hour. Blend
the flour to a smooth cream with a
tablespoonful or so of water and add
it to the sauce, stirring carefully. Add
the vegetable extract or ketchup and
a little gravy colouring to make it a
good rich brown. Re-season if necessary, and boil up before serving.

(Continued on page 100)

has approved these Recipes

WHAT I have to say this month may shock you. But I hope it won't. I hope instead you will face up to the problems which I am going to raise, particularly if you are the mother of a young, inexperienced girl.

Open on my desk is a letter. It is from a deeply distressed woman, the mother of a girl not yet seventeen. The girl is pregnant. Through the heartbroken lines of the mother's letter I can hear the cry, "*My* daughter, *my* daughter," echoing with grieving incredulity.

The girl is well-educated, carefully nurtured. The mother says, "She is so quiet, so happy at home that I have to *force* myself to believe that this has happened to her. I blame myself because I yielded to her patriotic desire to leave school and take a job. I see now that, straight from school, straight from her home, the risks were too many in these days when moral standards are so terribly lax."

with tragedy because so many parents refuse to discuss or even to recognise the social dangers into which these children are thrown.

It is an extraordinary paradox that, although for so many years we have been accustomed to frankness about sex, we still baulk at discussing the ugly but imperative aspects of it with our own children.

No mother to-day dreads or feels self-conscious over explaining puberty or the processes of birth. Neither is she much disturbed or discountenanced if, after opening the subject, the youngster of twelve or thirteen says, "Oh, I know all about that old stuff." But there are very few women who, when the time comes, are prepared to go the few logical steps further and tell a girl simply, and without mincing words, the results of promiscuity both mental as well as physical.

Why is this? Because the mother turns from

TELL YOUR DAUGHTER THE

It is a pitiful letter and I will not quote any more of it, except one line: "Mothers are not awake to the dangers which surround their girls. They should be warned."

Indeed they should. The instinct, among women who have led pleasant, sheltered lives, is to shudder at the realities of war-time social problems and resolutely to shut their eyes against the possibilities of their own children being affected by them. This is the easiest thing to do. This is the behaviour which is expected of them when the subject is broached with hushed voices among a few intimates.

Disgusting. Terrible. Shocking. In such terms is illicit sexual intercourse dismissed, together with the consequences, which may be the open disgrace of pregnancy, or the hidden one of venereal disease in one of its forms. Almost inevitably the subject is finally closed with the smug assumption that "of course, only a certain class is affected."

But facts show that this is not the case. Since the outbreak of the war, the problems of the illegitimate child and the occurrence of disease have touched alike the educated and the uneducated classes. The reason is not difficult to find: youth, drawn from every strata of society, is in the centre of the war-effort. Rather than remain at school, where they would normally be glad to stay, they are surging out into industry, gallantly eager to work for their country for which they are too young to fight. Their effort is magnificent, and it is pitiful that it should be edged

what she feels is crudity and hopes that the girl's natural instinct will save her. In the case of a timid or sensitive temperament this instinct may be a safeguard, although not an infallible one, but when a girl is endowed with vitality and a sense of adventure, it is still more vital that she should be well armoured against life by knowledge.

We still confuse ignorance with innocence. No girl, however retiring or gently romantic, can be harmed by knowledge if it is presented to her clearly and with dignity. She may, for the time being, feel shocked, but she will never forget, and, if she should find herself in danger of overstepping social bounds, that knowledge will return to her. Through it she will be able to estimate the true value of the attraction she feels and, unless she is one of those unhappy, but comparatively rare mortals, without natural standards, she will turn away from danger, realising that what is being offered to her by the man is neither fair or right.

I talked to a father of a girl the other day who was brought up in Paris. "I never had any fears for Jean," he said, "although she was so attractive that people noticed her everywhere, because her mother and I told her everything. We told her what might happen to her body if she permitted herself freedom with men; we told her what might happen if she drank too many cocktails. She was interested and sometimes startled by what we told her, but we knew she filed away the information. When she went out to parties

Make "Digging, Saving, Reaping, Keeping" your gardening motto.

we didn't impose any rulings about getting home, but we did say that personally we didn't advise this or that. As a consequence, and because we didn't try to force her by parental authority, she accepted our judgments. Now she's happily married, and a better wife, and companion than if she'd gone into matrimony knowing nothing of life.''

Those parents were wise, indeed. And girls living and working in war-time conditions, with those frequent flashes of false excitement and glamour, need such knowledge desperately. Far from spoiling their illusions, it will

TRUTH

enable them to keep them, because they will be equipped to judge the integrity of the men they meet, and enable them to estimate and respect the value of their own personalities and bodies. So many girls who are never told of their own value as potential wives and mothers, overlook it. All they are conscious of is the reckless thrill of youth, the excitement of being desired. They are blinded and trapped by their ignorance, not by their freedom or their knowledge.

The instinct to mate, to know physical love, is natural, and those who pretend to be disgusted by it are foolish. The duty of parents is to teach their girls to control this instinct until it can be fulfilled in its highest sense. This can only be done, not by restricting liberty or hiding the truth, but by giving a girl a simple and clean statement of facts before she goes out into the world.

If your girl is leaving school, or has just left school to take a war job, make this your first duty. It is cruel and dangerous to neglect it.

Puppy Love
IS THE REAL THING
By
Howard Whitman

REMEMBER when you were sixteen and you fell in love with the boy next door? Remember how your mother said, " Don't be silly—you're still a baby ''?

And the boy's father probably laughed and said to him: '' So it's puppy love, is it? Why son, you're still wet behind the ears! ''

This is the usual pattern. Most of us have Puppy Love pegged in our minds as something to make fun of. The reaction is almost automatic—like laughing when someone falls downstairs, even though it isn't funny.

Perhaps Puppy Love isn't funny either. Perhaps the joke has been on us. We may have overlooked some vital undercurrents beneath the comic surface that Puppy Love presents. And in overlooking, perhaps we've done some unintended harm.

Is Puppy Love fundamentally different from any other kind of romantic love? It is boy-girl attraction. The boy and the girl want to be together, they thrill in each other's presence, and they write strange little notes, often with private expressions that have meaning only for them.

Sounds familiar, doesn't it? For it is the same old formula which, with variations, spells love at any age—sixteen, twenty-six, or forty. But Puppy Love is more aboveboard than the rest. Its phenomena often manifest themselves openly: hearts and Cupid's darts on the covers of schoolbooks, big initials pencilled on the blotter, telephone calls that last an hour and twenty minutes.

Puppy Lovers are too young to get married. If they were five years older, perhaps they would wed and live happily ever after. The thing that is wrong is the timing; but the love is pretty much the same.

Grown folks, steeped in the habit of saying, '' Tut, tut, a mere case of puppy love,'' are prone to forget what the motives and ingredients of Puppy Love are.

There's an ample amount of wholesome hero worship. Perhaps your daughter has fallen in love with the best-looking boy in her set, or the best athlete. Or perhaps your son is in love with the girl who had the leading rôle in the Dramatic Society's last production.

Idealism is another ingredient. The young girl on her restless pillow of adolescence has dreamed of a handsome prince, clean-cut, manly, strong, virtuous, who is going to carry her away some day. In Puppy Love she feels she has found that dream person. And the boy, starry-eyed perhaps, feels he has discovered an ethereal princess. *(Continued on page 65)*

1

2

4

5

CLOTHES RELATIONS

3

6

W ITH a coat, a suit and a dress you have the right clothes for any occasion, and though in these days of economising money and coupons most of us can buy only one of these items at a time, these two groups may suggest how you can build a foolproof wardrobe round one favourite garment. For instance, with a gay-coloured coat, choose a neutral suit, a black dress. Or if you prefer a black coat, wear a vivid dress under it, or a check suit in which black predominates. But remember, haphazard purchase of a garment that doesn't fit into your particular colour scheme *never* makes for good dressing.

1 A casually-cut moss-green wool coat with long revers. " Utility " Dereta from Dickins and Jones.

2 Classic tailored suit in string-coloured tweed. " Utility " model from Harvey Nichols.

3 Black wool dress with cleverly draped bodice, box pleats in front of skirt. Roter " Utility " from Marshall and Snelgrove.

4 Black wool redingote, snugly waisted, with two pockets and welted seams. Selincourt from Marshall and Snelgrove.

5 Sage-green jersey shirt-dress with inverted pleat in skirt. Wolsey from the Inexpensive Dress Department at Harrods.

6 A suit for town or country in red, black and white check tweed, with deep box pleats in skirt. Harella " Utility " from D. H. Evans.

H—2

MARY GRAY writes with deep understanding for the wives who are expecting so much of the next precious " Seven Days "

THERE'S not a woman with a man in the Forces who does not know those exultant, expectant days before the long-awaited leave arrives. For wives, especially, they are days filled with dreaming and planning to make every moment perfect. Anticipation is in your heart and in your hands and beating behind your brain, so that it seems to carry you along on a forceful current at once unreal and tremendously real. Then the day arrives. He comes to you.

Sometimes everything is as lovely as you dreamed. It is as if there has been no interval of time, no long march of separate happenings since you last saw him. Time closes around you, shutting out the spaces of absence, admitting only harmony. And that's happiness, perfection; and marriage renewed with the bright, fresh colours of romance.

But sometimes, for all your planning and your hopes, this does not happen. You are puzzled and hurt. You blame the Service to which he belongs for taking him away from you and for building something into him during those weeks apart which you do not recognise. He's changed, you say, and you know there are tears behind your eyes, but you don't want him to see, because he would not understand and you would not be able to explain. What you feel is at once too complicated and too slight to put into words. You cannot feel close to him. There is no easy moving together of the mind, so that it is wonderful just to do nothing except potter around the house, knowing that if you call he will answer.

Depression starts like a little cold spot in your brain, because you are so desperately anxious that his leave should be happy, and depression grows into a frenzy. You try to fill with activity the gap you sense between you. You arrange for friends to come in, for him to go and see friends. You book seats at a theatre; order a table in a restaurant where you can dance. You feel if you only *do* enough, that queer reserve between you will dissolve.

But although he may fall in with your arrangements, you can tell he is lagging, not really enthusiastic. Something inside you gives up despairingly. You've done everything; hoped for everything, but it hasn't come out right, and you

wonder painfully if your marriage has not been spoilt by the war.

The mistake has been not in hoping and planning for happiness, but in trying to *force* it as you think it should be; in not having the determination to wait for him to settle down, when you first sense that the exquisite harmony is lacking. You have forgotten that a man coming home on leave has dreamed of that oasis in time as much as you, and that his emotions, like your own, are at concert pitch, so that the tiniest thing may throw them out of gear.

Women, even the most unselfish of us, are individualistic. Married and in love, we find it difficult to get it out of our heads that a man's happiness depends on our specially planned efforts. The more we love, the greater efforts we make during those brief reunions of leave. In our anxiety to please as we feel *should* please, we are apt to leave out one important consideration, *the state of mind of the man on whom we shower our devotion*.

As everyone knows who has been married in peace years, there are times when happiness can only be secured if the wife submerges her own impulsive wishes, her own very definite ideas. This is often still more vitally necessary when a man comes home on leave. Make your plans, live your hopes, but when you first meet him, try, for an hour or so, *(Continued on page* **92)**

HE'S COMING ON LEAVE

TURN THE HOUSE UPSIDE-DOWN AND THROW OUT YOUR SALVAGE

Francina Sorabji

P. Cornell

HOUSEWIVES SAVE YOUR SALVAGE

SALVAGE FOR VICTORY

Mary Greene

CHILDREN'S SALVAGE COMPETITION

THE entries in this contest were so good that we decided to increase the number of prizes in each class. We il-given in the lists on this page. We illustrate a few of those designs which lend themselves best to reproduction.

SALVAGE SPEEDS THE BOMBER

Ronald McRae

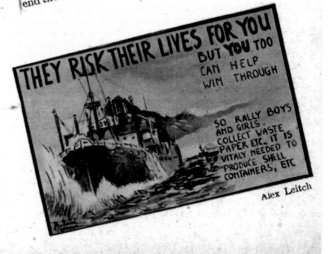

THEY RISK THEIR LIVES FOR YOU BUT YOU TOO CAN HELP WIN THROUGH SO RALLY BOYS AND GIRLS COLLECT WASTE PAPER ETC. IT IS VITALLY NEEDED TO PRODUCE SHELL CONTAINERS, ETC

Alex Leitch

Illustrated by Eric Fraser

"Lets talk

ONE great benefit which this war has brought to the people of Great Britain is the renewal of the habit of thinking. Everywhere, in cities, townships and villages, thought has come alive again, articulate and vigorous, and the source of this immensely important revival is to be found in Discussion Groups. These are now a hardy and progressive growth in most war-time organisations.

Before the war we were in grave danger of losing the power to think as individuals. We were becoming creatures of mass opinion over such wide, yet acutely personal fields as international politics, local government, home-planning, health services and entertainment. Some omnipotent power, without a name and without a shape, shouted at us what, in its own estimation, it would be best for us to have, and we had begun to accept these decrees with easy, but deadly dangerous clichés such as: "Well, perhaps it's for the best," or "It'll all be the same a hundred years from now." We were actually beginning to believe that what we thought and what we wanted did not matter, or rather *could* not matter.

But when the war came, we broke out of apathy with the biggest jolt we had known since the scarring years of 1914–18. Intense in our individual efforts to pursue this war unremittingly to victory, we became stabbed through with the consciousness of the power to think. Brought together at factory benches, in wardens' huts, in hostels, in the Services, in fact, in all places where people gather together to perform a common task, we began

to transform vague thoughts into concrete opinions and to address our minds to problems reasonably, but with determined coherence. Out of this renaissance, Discussion Groups were organised and have steadily become stronger and stronger, until now they are the ears and the tongue of the daily life of the people.

The National Fire Service took an early lead in this movement, which, although not new, has never been fully exploited to make its power and promise available to all. For over a year now, the N.F.S. has built up an expanding network of groups throughout its organisation. From the ranks of the service the organisers pick Group Leaders and give them a course of instruction at the City Literary Institute. These lectures do not seek to make public speakers of the Leaders, but to endow them, through psychology and logical thinking, with the ability to encourage others to think and talk. In addition, the Leaders have regular meetings at which they listen to authorities on subjects of the day.

Other organisations, although at the moment of writing they may not be so elaborately planned, are following the example of the N.F.S., and encouraging regular weekly meetings at which vital subjects can be talked over quietly and in the right perspective.

What are the subjects which attract the liveliest discussions? It is difficult to generalise, but an idea of their scope may be given by forming them into four main groups. These are:

1. The conduct of the war, both nationally and as it comes within the scope of local government.

2. The colossal home and international economic problems which are inevitable after the peace. Here people are asking, "What homes shall we live in?" "How shall we earn our bread and butter?" "What is the future of women in employment?"

3. The future of the Dominions, India, Russia, China and the United States, and their influence in Great Britain.

Don't take a chance—have your child inoculated against Diphtheria.

"*it over*"
By Margaret Pulsford

**Groups—a new kind of social activity that may [   ]
ideas on the world we're all wanting**

4. The ever-present topic of education and what the world will offer to the children now growing up, who will play such an enormous part in the progress and prosperity of the country.

Cynical people have been heard to question whether Discussion Groups have any real influence and whether any influence that may exist, can last.

I believe that such questioners are either too lazy to think for themselves, preferring to be directed by a central machine through which one can suffer as helplessly as one can profit, or else, possessing the capacity to think, they prefer apathetically, or with mistaken superiority, to withhold themselves from the struggles of the common people.

It is obvious to any keen-minded, optimistic and vigorous person that Discussion Groups are already having their influence, because through them ever-growing numbers of people are making their ideals and ambitions heard. This influence will continue to grow so long as the people have the will to keep their thoughts alive. That this will is undoubtedly alive now is witnessed by the millions who delight in the B.B.C. Brains Trust programmes, in which adolescents as well as adults take part, and by the fact that almost every week some new body adopts the principle of this group airing of opinions and problems and the exchange of ideas about them.

Youth Discussion Groups are steadily on the increase, and the Rev. J. Butterworth, who directs Clubland, the East End Settlement for boys and girls from sixteen to eighteen years old, told me that their "Weekly Parliament" is one of the most active branches of the organisation. It has a "Cabinet" composed of 28 members and a "House" of 200. The Prime Minister is elected every year, and the Cabinet comprises Rt. Hon. Members for Music, Drama, Boxing, Art and Economic Problems, such as London re-planning and slum clearance. Each week one or more subjects come up for debate, and various points of view are put forward as enthusiastically by girls as by boys.

Often I hear the remark, "Oh, I'd love to join a Group, but I'd feel so nervous of speaking, although there's such a lot I'd like to say." There is absolutely no necessity for this nervousness, because there is no question of formal speech-making. The Groups are simply a bunch of friends talking among themselves, as we so often do around our own firesides, or over the still more homely "back garden fence." Moreover, the discussions become so lively that a question or a remark on some aspect of living which is occupying your own mind seems to lift you up from your feet and voice itself! All you really have to do is to shape your thoughts so that they are disciplined and in logical sequence, and the more briefly you express them the better. As a Group Leader said to me, "The only qualification anybody needs is the willingness to think."

After all, how natural it is that Discussion Groups are daily becoming stronger, because what are they but the expression of our individuality in which, as a nation, we have always taken pride? It is because we are a nation of individuals that we have always been leaders towards higher ideas of world civilisation and universal freedom.

Admittedly, there must be a top group of leaders to direct the nation, but their efficiency depends, and always will, on the articulateness of the common people. Only by open discussion, undertaken by individuals as eager to learn as to voice their opinions, can those leaders understand how the majority want to be governed, and guide them towards the fulfilment of their aspirations.

During the last century we have undergone a change from autocracy to the idea of democracy through adult suffrage, but in the years before the war we were becoming indolent in the handling of our great advantages. The war jerked us back into  *(Continued on page 86)*

By Dilys Anthony

(*Combined Domestic Subjects Diploma, Berridge House, London*)

RAID Your Store

Use Bottled Fruit for:

1 Fruit Flans.

2 Fruit and Semolina Mould (see recipe).

3 Fruit Pies and Tarts.

4 Fruit Fools. Combine the sieved and sweetened fruit with an equal quantity of thick custard.

5 A Simple Sweet. Heat the fruit and serve it with creamed rice.

6 Mock Baba (see recipe).

7 Pears au Chocolat (see photograph, top right, and recipe.)

Use Tomatoes and Tomato Pulp for:

1 Soups (see recipe).

2 Sauces.

3 Macaroni Cheese. Place tomatoes in a greased pie-dish before pouring the macaroni cheese on top.

4 Tomato Savoury. Combine with a little flour and seasoning, stir until thick and boiling. Stir in grated cheese to taste and serve on toast or with mashed potatoes.

5 Tomato Creams (see recipe).

6 Savoury Tartlets (see recipe).

Use Apple Pulp for:

1 Wartime Marmalade—add skins from your children's oranges to the pulp (see recipe).

2 A Quick Sweet. Serve the pulp piled on slices of stale cake in individual glasses, with a teaspoonful of red jam on top.

3 "Mince" Tarts. To 1 lb. of apple pulp add about 2 oz. dried fruit, $\frac{1}{2}$ teaspoonful mixed spice, $\frac{1}{4}$ teaspoonful cinnamon and 2 teaspoonfuls golden syrup or sugar. Fill pastry cases with the mixture.

4 Apple Snow (see recipe).

5 Apple Amber (see photograph, right, and recipe).

Don't just gaze proudly at your bottled fruits and preserves. Open them, use them in interesting ways. Now is the time for which they were prepared

AND HERE ARE THE RECIPES:

Mock Baba

1-lb. bottle of fruit   Sugar to taste

Sponge Mixture	Sauce
2 oz. margarine	½ oz. flour (custard powder or
2 oz. sugar	cornflour gives a more
4 oz. flour	glossy sauce)
1 dried egg, reconstituted	½ pint fruit juice (or juice made up to
2 tablespoonfuls water	½ pint with water)
1 heaped teaspoonful	Sugar to taste
baking powder	Ginger or cinnamon

Strain the juice from the fruit. Cream the fat and the sugar very thoroughly, beat in the reconstituted egg and the water, fold in the flour and baking powder. Place this mixture in a greased ring mould and bake in a moderately hot oven (375° F.) for 30–35 minutes. Meanwhile make the sauce just as you would make custard, and add a little ground ginger or cinnamon. Turn the mould on to a hot plate, fill the centre with sweetened fruit and pour the hot sauce over it. Decorate the top with a little more fruit.

This same recipe can be used for making Eve's Pudding. The strained fruit is then placed at the bottom of a greased pie-dish and the creamed mixture on top. Bake in a moderately hot oven (375° F.) for 40–45 minutes till golden-brown and firm. Use the juice to make a sauce to serve with it.

Apple Amber

6 oz. shortcrust pastry

Filling

1-lb. bottle of apple pulp	1–2 dried eggs (used dry)
1 oz. margarine	A little lemon flavouring
1–2 oz. sugar	A little mock cream

Make the pastry and line a deep pie plate with it. Bake in a hot oven. Pour the apple pulp into a saucepan and bring to boiling point. Stir in the sugar, margarine and flavouring. Sift in the dried egg powder and boil for 2 or 3 minutes to cook the egg. Beat well till smooth. Pile into the pastry case, and serve hot or cold. If to be served cold, pipe mock cream round or pile on top, to give the appearance of whites of eggs. (Continued on page 106)

Pears au Chocolat (above) may be piped with whipped cream for festive occasions. Apple Amber (right) is good either alone or in a flan

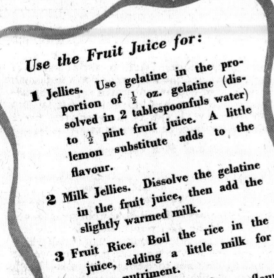

Use the Fruit Juice for:

1 **Jellies.** Use gelatine in the proportion of ½ oz. gelatine (dissolved in 2 tablespoonfuls water) to ½ pint fruit juice. A little lemon substitute adds to the flavour.

2 **Milk Jellies.** Dissolve the gelatine in the fruit juice, then add the slightly warmed milk.

3 **Fruit Rice.** Boil the rice in the juice, adding a little milk for extra nutriment.

4 **Sauces.** Proportions are ½ oz. flour to ½ pint juice. Specially good with fruit-stuffed pancakes.

Tested and Recommended by GOOD HOUSEKEEPING INSTITUTE

1 Begin by collecting everything you'll need for your home shampoo—hair tonic, shampoo, grips, pins, curlers, setting lotion and net, brush and comb. Next, remove dust and any particles of dead skin from the hair and scalp by giving the hair a thorough brushing. Comb out the tangles, then, keeping the head low so that the vitalising blood rushes to the scalp, brush up and away from the hair-lines. Start at the nape of the neck and brush up to the crown, brush upwards from the temples, and, finally, from the forehead—a hundred strokes in all.

2 If your hair is dry or lustreless, now is the time to give it an oil treatment. Heat some oily-type tonic by standing the bottle in a saucepan of hot water, then with a piece of cotton-wool swab the warm oil down a series of partings until the whole head has been covered. Knead the scalp gently, moving it rather than the fingers, and work from hair-lines to crown. Now wring out a thick towel in very hot water and wind this round the head to open the pores of the scalp and enable it to absorb the oil in the shortest possible time.

3 Prepare your shampoo according to the directions, divide it into two parts and, if you have given yourself the oil treatment, rinse the hair with cold water to float off the oil, adding a pinch of borax

FIVE-STEP

to each rinsing water. Massage the first half of the shampoo well into the head and rinse off with clear water. Pour on the second half, rub it well into the scalp, and don't forget the ends, or the temple and forehead hair. Rinse in four or five waters, after which the hair should "squeak" between the fingers. If you catch cold easily, finish with a cold rinse, but hair with a slight natural curl sets more easily if the last rinse is hot. If the hair is oily, or

Now turn to page 49 for FRANCES LORING'S helpful answers to your Beauty problems

if there is a tendency to dandruff, this is a good time to give the hair a tonic treatment. Part-dry the hair with a warm towel, saturate the scalp with your spirit-type tonic, antiseptic hair lotion or bay rum, sprinkling it down a series of partings, then follow the massage directions given to those with dry hair. A second application of tonic should be used for setting.

SHAMPOO

By
Susan Drake

Hair which has not been given a tonic treatment should be saturated with setting lotion.

4 To set the hair, make your parting, pinch in your waves and roll the ends of the hair into disc curls. To make a wave, comb (Continued on page 101)

When Girdles Fail

By Susan Drake

HOW is your girdle area? Now that you can no longer get your pet rubberised, figure-moulding girdle, or rely on your belt to tailor your figure, how are you going to achieve the pencil-slim silhouette with which we are threatened, or even maintain reasonably good measurements? Well, you must extend your mend-and-make-do activities to cover your figure as well as your frock, and do your own figure-tailoring.

There are five danger-spots, or, as it appears from your letters, five depressing areas. They are: the diaphragm roll or spare tyre—that ugly roll of flesh just above the waist; a tummy which is not as flat as it might be; spreading hips—those pannier-like pads of flesh on the upper hips; the posterior or bustle effect; and heavy, bulging thighs. Let's tackle them in turn.

SPARE TYRE

See that your belt comes well above the rib cage. The roll-on belt which finishes just below the ribs is apt to make an ugly groove, pushing up the flesh to form a roll at the waistline.

Learn to stand with the muscles at the waistline pulled in. Put your hands lightly on your waist just beneath the ribs, take a deep breath and feel how your hands sink in. Now pull in the muscles while breathing normally. Do this consciously for a few minutes each day, increasing the time gradually. When your muscles are under control, you'll do it without thinking about it.

Massage will help to reduce the roll, provided it is done regularly. Pinch around the front of your waistline every day when dressing and undressing, continuing until the skin is pink.

Exercise

Stand feet apart, arms stretched out at shoulder level. Keeping the knees straight, bend and touch the left toe with the fingers of the right hand, swinging the left arm up and behind. Straighten up, and bend to the right, touching the toe of right foot with left hand. Repeat ten times, breathing *in* as you straighten up, *out* as you bend. (Fig 1.)

TUMMY TROUBLE

Even a slightly bulging tummy can spoil your silhouette and make your frock sit badly. If this is your problem, make sure that your elimination is good, and that you sit and stand tall, with the bust up and the waist well out of your rib cage.

When breathing deeply or step-breathing, let the breath out slowly between pursed lips. This helps to strengthen the tummy muscles. Incidentally, step-breathing—breathing deeply to a count of eight steps—if done regularly each day when walking to bus or train, is one of the best ways there is of keeping influenza and the common cold at bay.

Exercise

Lie flat with the knees straight and the feet together. Now lift the head from the floor as if to look at your toes, and at the same time move the toes upwards towards the head. Let the head fall back and the toes return to their original position. Repeat ten times. (Fig. 2.) Still lying flat, draw your knees up and at the same time lift your head from the floor as if you hoped to touch chin and knees. Repeat ten times. (Fig. 3.)

HIP-SPREAD

Keep your knees together as much as possible when sitting or walking. If you are walking correctly, with one foot in front of the other and not in parallel lines, the knees will brush each other lightly. If you sit with the knees wide apart, the muscles at the back are stretched in the wrong way, and this helps the hip-line to spread.

Those with hippy figures should watch their diet, go easy with starchy food and try to have one starch-free meal each day—a clear vegetable soup, perhaps, followed by a salad or a vegetable dish and stewed fruit.

Always give the hips an extra rub-a-dub with a rough towel or friction glove after bath or wash. Anything which brings the blood rushing to the surface of the skin helps to get rid of superfluous fat.

Exercise

Lie flat on the floor, place the hands palms downwards under the lower back, and bicycle, drawing the knees alternately towards the tummy and stretching each foot as high as possible. Continue while you count thirty, increasing the number each day until you are bicycling for a full two minutes. (Fig. 4.)

THE BUSTLE LINE

Fat on the buttocks ruins the effect of a tailored suit, but it is a comparatively easy fault to correct. The first thing is to learn to stand and walk correctly with the tail tucked in. Don't try to contract the tail muscles. Stand erect, slacken the knees and throw the hips forward, and as the spine straightens, the tail will automatically fall into place.

Try to find a belt with a non-stretch panel across the back, and always smooth the flesh of the buttocks sideways and down before fastening it.

Exercise

Standing with the knees flexed, slightly sideways to wall or cupboard, whack the posterior against the hard surface, allowing the fleshiest part (not the kidney region) to take the beating. Don't stop till you've had fifty good whacks on either side. (Fig. 5.)

BULGING THIGHS

A belt which comes low down over the thighs is, of course, ideal, but if you can no longer buy one, see that your girdle is not tight enough to force the thighs into an ugly, bulging ridge.

Deep pinching massage, with or without a reducing preparation, will slim the thighs, but it must be done for ten minutes night and morning. Failing a reducing cream or lotion, use talc, and work from knee to hip, pinching, kneading and slapping the flesh.

Exercise

Lying on back, shoulders flat on floor, knees bent, tummy indented and tail slightly raised off the floor, roll both knees to the left side with a good hard spank. Return to original position and drop them over to the right. Repeat fifty times. This also reduces hips and seat. (Fig. 6.)

FOR THE LAZY

Perhaps all your girdle region needs attention, but all that you will be persuaded to do is just one exercise. Then here's the one for you—it will help to slim that whole area.

Exercise

Sit on the floor, legs straight in front of you, feet together, arms stretched forward. Now roll back on your right shoulder-blade. Come back to your original position and roll on to your left, keeping the hands off the floor and the ankles together, and coming back to the place where you started. Repeat until you have done thirty to fifty rolls. (Fig. 7.)

You are as young as *Your Hair* * Your

AGE-GUESSING is a favourite game of mine. I'm pretty good at it; but when I'm doubtful, I turn to four points about a woman:

Your Hair

Young hair is well-nourished hair. When the hair becomes scanty, brittle, lank or streaky, you can be pretty sure that the circulation of the head has slowed down and the hair is on a starvation diet.

Rush nourishment to the hair by stimulating the circulation of the head. Double your hair-brush drill, brushing up, up, up from the headlines. Massage the scalp to loosen it. A tight scalp is an ageing scalp. Rest the elbows on a table with the tips of the fingers pressed on the scalp and the thumbs behind the ears. Move the whole head in an anti-clockwise direction, keeping the fingers still, but moving the scalp.

By Susan Drake

Throat ★ Your Eyes ★ Your Hands

Hair falls in the spring, and this is the time to nourish the new hair by treating yourself to a good hair tonic, massaging it into your head every other day for a month. There are some excellent tonics which may still be had. Failing one, use one part castor oil with three parts Eau de Cologne.

Change your hair parting and change your hair style. The woman who clings to the same hair-do, year in, year out, dates herself relentlessly. Beware of hair that is too heavy, too thick, for that gives an old-fashioned look to the head. The modern head is thinned out and the hair tapered not less often than every three months.

Your Throat

Good posture, regular exercise for muscles of jaw and throat, lubrication and stimulation—these are the secrets of a youthful throat. Keep your head up and your eyes level when you sit, walk or stand. Practise walking with a heavy book on your head. Imagine that that book is still there as you walk down the street, and at night sleep on a low pillow.

For the plump throat and double chin there are two simple exercises which you can do at odd moments. (1) Curl your tongue towards the back of the throat, keep it there while you count ten, and relax. (2) Rest your elbows on a table, take chin in hands and slowly force open your mouth against the pressure of your hands.

If the throat is thin and lined, blow out a row of imaginary candles half a dozen times a day, and open your mouth in a huge yawn, tilt back your head, stifle the yawn and slowly lower the head.

Crêpy skin on the throat means that the skin needs stimulation. Wind a series of hot towels round the neck until the skin is pink, cover the throat with cream and, clenching your fists, use the knuckles like animated rollers, walking them up the neck, knuckle by knuckle, till the chin is reached. Now work along the jaw-line to the ears. Start again from the centre of the throat, and go over the entire neck until the cream has been absorbed. Wet a pad of cotton-wool in skin tonic or cold water and slap the neck lightly.

Your Eyes

Be kind to those eyes of yours. Guard them from strain. To read in jolting vehicles, in a bad light, on your elbow in bed, or without glasses when you need them, is to age them rapidly. If you live in a dusty city or use mascara, bathe them lightly with eye lotion; and whenever you have a few minutes to relax, close them under pads of cotton-wool soaked in warm milk or cool eye lotion. Use odd moments to relax them by blinking, to place your palms over your closed lids and "see" black, to dart your eyes hither and thither and circle them widely while keeping the head still.

Keep the skin round the eyes smooth by keeping it well lubricated. Don't use too much cream, or it will seep into the eyes and make them puffy. A piece of cream the size of a large pea is sufficient for the skin round both eyes. (Continued on page 57)

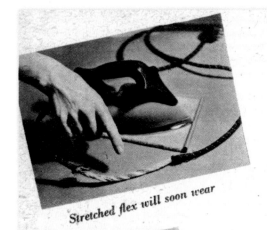
Stretched flex will soon wear

Your Electric

The small electrical appliances in your home will serve you well—if you take care of them. Dampness and rough usage quickly ruin insulation, so handle all appliances carefully and keep flexes away from moisture, unless they are rubber-covered. Don't let water drip into electric connections.

Wind the cord loosely

Your iron.—It will give you better service and last longer if you keep it clean and avoid overheating it. The flex should never be stretched or wound round a hot iron. Keep a look-out for a worn flex and have it repaired as quickly as possible.

Your vacuum cleaner.—Empty the dust bag after every use—a choked bag puts a strain on the motor and reduces efficiency of the cleaner. Never wash the bag, but clean it thoroughly with a small whisk brush. Don't pick up broken glass or pins with a vacuum cleaner. Keep brushes clean and check the cord and connections often. Never wind the cord tightly after using the cleaner—tight winding shortens its life.

Your refrigerator.—De-frost it regularly. Keep all moist foods covered, otherwise de-frosting will be necessary more often. Don't put warm foods in the refrigerator; it wastes current and means unnecessary condensation. Never leave the door open unless the appliance is being put out of use for some time. Wash the inside regularly with lukewarm water containing a little baking soda.

Your lighting.—An old, blackened lamp is a current waster. Keep lamps and fittings clean—dirty shades waste a great deal of light. Use portable low-wattage lamps where possible, so that you can bring the light close to your work.

Your electric cooker.—Wipe over oven immediately after use with a damp cloth, and occasionally wipe the boiling-plates with an oily rag. To keep free from grease, periodically clean the inside of the oven with a cloth wrung out in hot water to which soda has been added.

Use " low heat " whenever possible, and don't waste current and time by using the grill boiler for boiling unless it is also in use for grilling. Remember always to switch off current before cleaning.

Bring the light to your work

Your electric toaster.—If it has a removable base, take this out and brush out the crumbs with a soft brush. Never use a knife or the prongs of a fork. A heavy accumulation of crumbs round the heating unit can cause a blown fuse. Never immerse the toaster in water and don't shake it vigorously, as this may loosen the wires.

Kettle.—If you live in a hard-water district, de-fur your kettle at intervals. The simplest way is to fill it with lukewarm water and then add 2 tablespoonfuls of vinegar to each pint of water. Leave to stand 3 or 4 hours, empty out and rinse thoroughly. Repeat treatment if necessary.

Use low heat when you can

Servants

De-frost regularly

Your electric fires. The heating element is usually wound on to a fire-clay "bar" or rod. To clean the fire, use a soft brush or blow any dust out with a vacuum cleaner and then wipe the exterior with a soft cloth. If an electric fire or other apparatus is used in the bathroom, it is vitally important never to touch it with wet hands, and it should be so placed that it cannot be reached from the bath. In new housing schemes a ceiling switch with a pull cord is advocated for safety-first reasons.

Mechanical apparatus.—This is often misused in the home, but if an electric motor is to give long and satisfactory service, it should be looked after. Avoid overheating or overtaxing the motor by running appliances for too long a period continuously or by overloading. Take care, for instance, not to overstrain your electric washer by filling the tub with too many large articles at a time. It is better to wash one large sheet with smaller things, rather than to make up a complete load of big articles. Similarly with other pieces of mechanism—overstrain must be avoided if you want their life to be long and trouble-free.

Make Do and Mend

If you want individual help do not hesitate to call at Good Housekeeping Make Do and Mend Advice Centre or to write to the Institute.

From a colour film taken at the Institute

G.H. ACTIVITIES

INSTITUTE DEMONSTRATIONS—JUNE

Preservation of Fruit and Vegetables. Three demonstrations to be given on Thursdays at 3 p.m. Admission, 3s. 6d. each.

June 8th, *Jam-making.*—Principles of Preservation. Jam and jelly making. Low-sugar jams. Pectin extracts and their use. Methods of covering.

June 15th, *Fruit Bottling.*—Bottling of fruit by various methods. Types of jars and covers. Fruit pulps and syrups. Use of sulphur-dioxide.

June 22nd, *Vegetable Preservation.*—Pickles and chutneys. Salting of beans. Drying of fruit, vegetables and herbs. Bottling of vegetables—use of pressure cooker.

The above course will be repeated on Thursday evenings at 6 p.m., on July 6th, 13th and 20th. Admission 3s. 6d. each.

Salad Days. A special Demonstration showing the preparation of a variety of salads, English and Continental, with suitable dressings and sauces: Wednesday, June 14th, at 3 p.m. Admission 3s. 6d., including afternoon tea.

Luncheon Dishes. A good selection of savoury and sweet dishes for warm weather. First of a series of Wednesday lunch-time demonstrations: June 28th, 1.5 p.m. to 1.45 p.m. Admission 2s. 6d., including light luncheon.

At Good Housekeeping Lecture Hall, 30 Grosvenor Gardens, London, S.W.1. Telephone, Sloane 4591.

SCHOOL OF CANTEEN COOKERY

The Good Housekeeping Diploma is a useful certificate of proficiency awarded to men and women who have successfully passed their examinations in Household and Canteen Cookery.

Household Cookery and Dietetics : 9.30 a.m. to 4 p.m., Monday to Friday. Six-week Diploma Course, fee 13 guineas. (This course may be studied without taking the final examination, if preferred.)

Canteen Cookery and Management : 8.30 a.m. to 4 p.m., Monday to Friday. Six-week Diploma Course, fee 13 guineas. This course includes practical experience in the Meals Centre attached to the School, where Students serve up to 300 lunches daily to the public between 12 noon and 2 p.m.

Combined Household and Canteen Training : Twelve-week Diploma Course, fee £25.

Refresher Courses in Canteen Cookery (no Diplomas given) may be taken at 2 guineas per week.

Evening Classes in Household Cookery : (*Basic*) Tuesday evenings, 6–8 p.m. (*More Advanced*) Thursday evenings, 6–8 p.m. Fee, 2½ guineas per 13 lessons. Other evenings by arrangement.

At Good Housekeeping School of Canteen Cookery, 30 Grosvenor Gardens, London, S.W.1. Telephone Sloane 4591.

Keep simmering for another 15 minutes before removing.

*Below:
the style adopted
for
" Casablanca "*

*Below:
" For Whom the Bell
Tolls " demands
a simple style*

*In · " Saratoga Trunk "
Miss Bergman looked like
this—gay and sophisticated*

*Miss Bergman
in " Adam Had
Four Sons ".*

*As the devoted
wife in
" Rage in Heaven "*

One Woman ~ SIX

IF every man has "two soul-sides," then every woman has at least six facets to her personality. Think a minute! Aren't there some who think of you as gay and frivolous, at least one man for whom you spell romance, someone to whom you are everything that is soft and feminine, another to whom you are the practical business woman, or an unspoiled, unsophisticated girl?

Now that we can no longer change our surroundings, see new people, wear new frocks, or even buy a new lipstick very often, it's fun to present a new face to our world, to the circle which may affectionately be taking us too much for granted. Leaving others aside, a new reflection in the mirror is a tonic to any woman. We can achieve a new face by changing our hair-styles, and the transformation which a hair-style can make in a woman's looks is illustrated by these six pictures of Ingrid Bergman.

● Opposite you see Miss Bergman as she appeared in *Casablanca*, with shoulder-length hair arranged in loose waves and curls. In my opinion, this is a style which should not be worn after the early twenties, and it is not a practical one in wartime. Though it is a feminine and glamorous style for stage and screen, it is not nearly as casual as it looks, and needs far more expert attention than the majority of us can give today.

● Miss Bergman wore a very different style in *Saratoga Trunk*. This is a party style, slick, gay, perfect for the woman with the longish face, and for all but the very young. The hair is brushed up from the temples, and the front hair is given a deep wave and the ends arranged in disc curls. When the hair is dry these ends are combed out over the fingers to form what is known as a tailored bang or fringe. The hair should be from eight to ten inches long for this style.

● Also on the opposite page you see her as she appeared in *For Whom the Bell Tolls*. She is wearing a practical upswept style specially designed for the busy woman. With slight adaptation it can be worn by most types, though it is seen at its best

Ingrid Bergman as she appears in her new film " Gaslight "

when the features are strongly marked, or unusually piquante. Have the hair tapered to an all-over length of four inches, and unless the hair is naturally curly, you must have a permanent wave, a point-winding one, so that the hair curls from the tip up to the scalp.

● As the devoted wife in *Rage in Heaven*, Miss Bergman wore a simple hair-do, the hair brushed smoothly across her brow with just the faintest ripple of a wave. If this is to be successful, it must, like all simple styles, be crisply clean and shining with health and brushing. This, too, is an under-twenty- (Continued on page 76)

FACES

by
Susan Drake

H—3

Scenes from three Coward plays — "Design for Living," "This Happy Breed," "Blithe Spirit"

In May we published a study by an English writer of the distinguished American actors, Lynn Fontanne and Alfred Lunt, in their current success, "There Shall be No Night." Read now an American's view of their closest English friend—

By
Ward Morehouse

NOEL

THERE was a period following Great Britain's declaration of war during which Noel Coward, the world's jack-of-all-entertainment, gave his friends cause for alarm: he came dangerously near pomposity. As so very many other artistes have done throughout the drama's unheeding years, he said his good-bye to the theatre, proclaiming, with a most unbecoming solemnity, that he was through with it for the duration. He began dabbling in international politics and was forever being whisked away on missions that were mysteriously official. He took his Martinis in Government Houses and took himself seriously while sipping them. He became something of a self-appointed High Ambassador to Practically Everything, and began filling a war-time rôle somewhat akin to that which had belonged to the Prince of Wales in bygone years.

Fortunately, however—and fortunately indeed for bored, restless and entertainment-hungry Allied troops on ever-alerted but inactive fronts—Noel happily recovered. With a twitch of his impudent and expressive eyebrows and probably a Cowardesque grimace or two, he got hold of himself, laughed convulsively at himself, begged the drama's forgiveness for his neglect, and returned forthwith to the only job he knew and knows —entertaining. He began visiting camps, bases, hospitals and troop concentrations here, there and everywhere to give his one-man show—songs in his fashion, and at whatever piano they happened to have around; stories in his clipped, laconic, amusingly venomous way, never avoiding impish malice when it could be used to humorous advantage, and autographing and hand-shaking to the steady accompaniment of his own crisp chatter, his

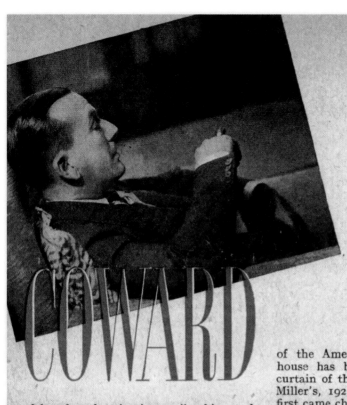

COWARD

delayed and quivering smile, his cruel-lipped and darting twists of speech.

He has given his concerts, as he calls them, throughout the British Isles and the vast Mediterranean area—Gibraltar, Malta, Algiers, Cairo, the Suez Canal zone, and in such Near East points as Teheran and Bagdad, that dusty and over-glamorised city cleft by the muddy Tigris. He has been the theatre's and his country's royal funmaker in Australia and South Africa. He has dropped out of the sky to do his highly specialised act for the maimed and the wounded in scores of hospitals, always finding himself greatly moved by the courage and cheerfulness of the shattered young men of modern war, and never failing to become somewhat disturbed and apologetic about his own non-combatant rôle, with its attendant health, wealth and security. As a government emissary on undisclosed and unrehearsed missions he became actually stuffy, and was probably among the first to be aware of it. But as a troop-entertainer paying impromptu calls on fighting-men in remote corners of the globe, he is in his own *métier*, contributing vitally to the war effort. In such capacity he will continue until the war is over. And then?

Noel Coward, actor, playwright, lyricist, composer, raconteur and world-traveller, will be forty-five in December. He has written farces, comedies, dramas, revues and operettas and has composed countless songs. His forty to fifty plays have included whopping hits, such as *Private Lives, Bitter Sweet, This Year* of *Grace, Design for Living, The Vortex* and *Blithe Spirit*, by far his most successful piece of writing to date. In *Cavalcade* he gave the theatre a stirring, patriotic panorama of British history, and Coward fans all the way from Boston to Bombay heard that he was to be knighted in recognition of such service, but nothing ever came of it.

In the war-time film *In Which We Serve*, which won the New York screen critics' prize as the best film of 1942, he was extraordinarily successful in a medium for which he professes to have neither talent nor interest. He has never been madly keen, as he might put it, to go in for screen acting or writing or producing more than casually.

He is a dramatist who has been booed on his own first nights—booed certainly when *Sirocco* had its London première—and given ovations that have shaken Shaftesbury Avenue —and New York's Forty-third Street, too. For there have been few nights in the history of the American stage when the tumult within a playhouse has been equal to that which came at the final curtain of the New York opening of *The Vortex* at Henry Miller's, 1925. There have been several periods, since he first came challengingly to the front as a man of the theatre who could do practically anything, when both London and New York have been seized by epidemics of his plays. At one stage and phase of his career he had playwriting contracts to supply the clamorous needs of fifteen managers, and to do it more or less simultaneously.

All of which makes it difficult to blend this picture with that of the Noel Coward of three and twenty years ago who, as a flippant (Continued on page 51)

Noel Coward in
" Present Laughter "

DRY SWIMMING

1
More oxygen in the lungs means greater vitality and joy of living. Fill the basin with water. Place a mirror at the bottom. Turn head to side as shown. Open mouth wide and take in a big gulp of air. Then turn face into the water, keeping eyes open, and breathe slowly out through the nose. Your eyes being open, you can of course see the air bubbles forming in the water.

2
Do the Breast Stroke Dry Swim to build up the upper part of the chest. Stand with head erect, eyes looking straight ahead, arms raised as shown. Now swing arms slowly back on a line with shoulders. Finish by bending elbows and bringing hands back to position in front of chest, ready to move forward again.

5
The Side Stroke is fine for slimming heavy legs. Stretch right arm straight, sliding left arm up in front of chest until it reaches your face, then sweeping it down to hip. Right arm goes forward as left arm goes back to hip. Legs are opened and closed like scissors—under leg is bent back at knee, while upper leg goes forward with knee unbent. Reverse the motions on left side.

Hang your clothes on the back of a chair—and don't go

near the water, says a famous American

swimming authority, VICTOR LAWSON

YOU don't need to give up slimming even if you can't get near the sea-shore this year. Try Dry Swimming—the simple way to keep fit throughout the year.

Dry Swimming, this smart, modern method of streamlining the figure and building muscles, is sponsored by many doctors as a means of benefiting patients who are over-weight from inactivity, and of stimulating and re-developing tired muscles.

3 This is how you may practise the Breast Stroke Dry Swim with arms and legs together. Try this while lying across a bench. Bend legs back, keeping heels together. Then throw legs out—right leg to right side and left leg to left side—finishing with legs straight together.

4 Now try Dry Swimming the Crawl. Begin by walking briskly around the room, arms swinging vigorously. You are almost doing the Crawl. Now lie over on your bench. Move arms, alternately, forward and back to hip, and sway legs up and down, alternately, from the hips. Keep feet slightly pigeon-toed: this strengthens arches and ankles.

6 The English Relaxation position has been filmed under Mr. Lawson's direction for the Government, to demonstrate to war-workers this essential aid to health. Lie still in this position when you feel tired. In a few moments your tired muscles will relax, and you will feel refreshed.

7 Mr. Lawson's method of Dry Swimming the American Back Crawl was adopted by a Fifth Avenue beauty salon as a means of developing that good posture so sought after as an essential to beauty, poise and confidence.

Vary your strokes from day to day. Allow five minutes for each stroke.

DRIED EGG PROBLEMS

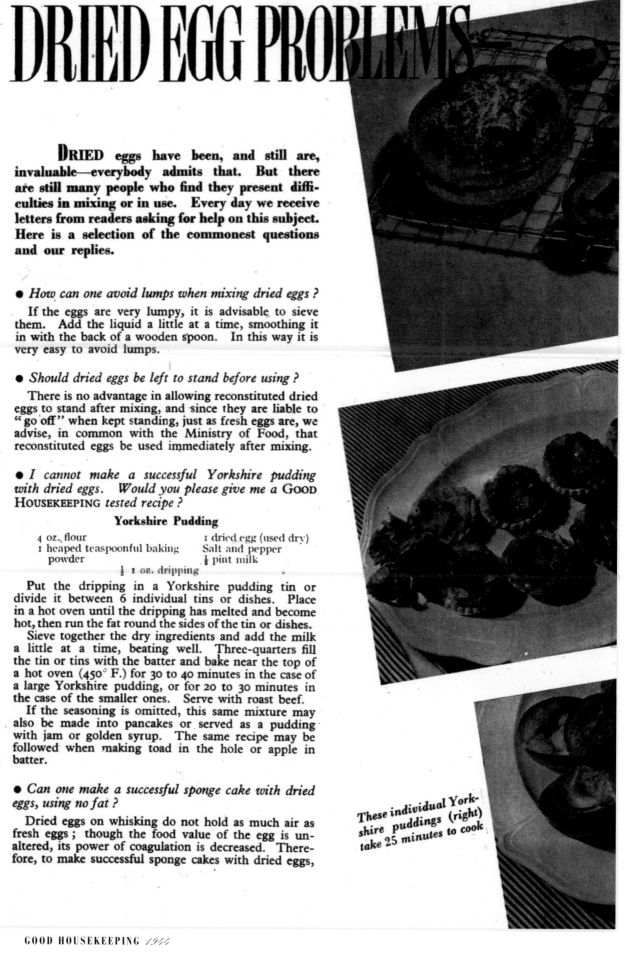

DRIED eggs have been, and still are, invaluable—everybody admits that. But there are still many people who find they present difficulties in mixing or in use. Every day we receive letters from readers asking for help on this subject. Here is a selection of the commonest questions and our replies.

● *How can one avoid lumps when mixing dried eggs ?*

If the eggs are very lumpy, it is advisable to sieve them. Add the liquid a little at a time, smoothing it in with the back of a wooden spoon. In this way it is very easy to avoid lumps.

● *Should dried eggs be left to stand before using ?*

There is no advantage in allowing reconstituted dried eggs to stand after mixing, and since they are liable to "go off" when kept standing, just as fresh eggs are, we advise, in common with the Ministry of Food, that reconstituted eggs be used immediately after mixing.

● *I cannot make a successful Yorkshire pudding with dried eggs. Would you please give me a* GOOD HOUSEKEEPING *tested recipe ?*

Yorkshire Pudding

4 oz. flour	1 dried egg (used dry)
1 heaped teaspoonful baking powder	Salt and pepper
	¼ pint milk

½ 1 oz. dripping

Put the dripping in a Yorkshire pudding tin or divide it between 6 individual tins or dishes. Place in a hot oven until the dripping has melted and become hot, then run the fat round the sides of the tin or dishes.

Sieve together the dry ingredients and add the milk a little at a time, beating well. Three-quarters fill the tin or tins with the batter and bake near the top of a hot oven (450° F.) for 30 to 40 minutes in the case of a large Yorkshire pudding, or for 20 to 30 minutes in the case of the smaller ones. Serve with roast beef.

If the seasoning is omitted, this same mixture may also be made into pancakes or served as a pudding with jam or golden syrup. The same recipe may be followed when making toad in the hole or apple in batter.

● *Can one make a successful sponge cake with dried eggs, using no fat ?*

Dried eggs on whisking do not hold as much air as fresh eggs ; though the food value of the egg is unaltered, its power of coagulation is decreased. Therefore, to make successful sponge cakes with dried eggs,

These individual York-shire puddings (right) take 25 minutes to cook

it is necessary to use a raising agent. Here is an excellent recipe :

Fatless Sponge Cake

2 dried eggs (reconstituted)	1 teaspoonful baking powder
3 oz. sugar	2 tablespoonfuls boiling water
3 oz. flour	Flavouring

Whisk the eggs, sugar and one-third of the flour over boiling water until thick and frothy (10 to 15 minutes). Sift the remaining flour and baking powder into the mixture, together with the boiling water and the flavouring. Fold in very lightly with a metal spoon. It is important to treat the mixture as gently as possible and to avoid stirring. If necessary, add a little more boiling water until the mixture is slack enough to pour easily. Pour immediately into two shallow tins or one deep one, previously prepared by greasing and lining with a round of greased paper. (This same mixture may be made into twelve small sponge cakes if liked. In this case the tins do not need to be lined with paper.) Bake in a hot oven (475° F.) for 7 to 10 minutes until well risen and golden brown. Turn on to a cake rack and allow to cool. If one deep sponge sandwich is being made, split it and spread a layer of jam in between. In the case of small cakes, if liked, the tops may be cut, a layer of jam placed on the cakes and the tops replaced, so making " top-hats."

● *My dried-egg custard does not thicken as well as one made with fresh eggs. How should it be made ?*

For cup custard, make a cornflour or custard-powder mixture, allowing 1 oz. of cornflour or custard powder to the pint of milk and two reconstituted dried eggs. Blend the cornflour or custard powder mixture with some of the milk. Bring the rest of the milk to the boil. Pour the boiling milk on to the blended cornflour. Add the reconstituted eggs, sugar to taste, and flavouring if liked. Return to the pan and stir over gentle heat until thick and boiling. In this case the custard may, of course, be boiled without any danger of the eggs curdling.

When making baked custards without any thickening ingredient, use two dried eggs to ½ pint milk. Reconstitute the eggs, stir in the hot milk and bake in the usual way.

● *How can I avoid a thick skin on the surface of a custard tart or baked custard ?*

When dried eggs are used for baked custard there is usually a thin skin on the surface when the custard is cooked. This is quite pleasant to eat. A thick skin means that the dried eggs have not been mixed carefully in the first place. (Continued on page 92)

Sponge cake mixture can be made into a sandwich cake, or into " top hat " queen cakes

Cheese tartlets, served cold with watercress for garnish

–Solved Here

By Dilys Anthony
(Combined Domestic Science Diploma, Burridge House, London)

The Ministry of Food has approved these recipes

Decorative Aprons: Unrationed canvas and hessian were used for these three good-looking aprons, though you could equally well make them in other plain fabrics. Choose bright, gay colours and skilfully contrasted embroidery. Full instructions for cutting, making and decorating all three aprons in Good Housekeeping Needlework Bulletin No. 133, price 1s. post free.

Make them...

Address your orders to : Good Housekeeping Needlework

Coupon-free Slippers: Soft, gaily-coloured "skivers" or piece-bag remnants of stout fabric are used for these practical slippers. Send 7d. in stamps, asking for Good Housekeeping Pattern No. 8 if you would like the children's slippers (pattern gives sizes 3–13), or 11d. for Pattern No. 9 if you wish to make the adults' wedge slippers (sizes 4–7 given, with instructions for adapting to larger sizes).

Something Embroidered: There are 12 large pages—29 x 9 ins.—of transfers, in the Good Housekeeping Embroidery Transfer Book. Thirty-seven designs are included, ranging from wildflower sprays suitable for lingerie to the handsome Queen Anne bowl of flowers shown last month and the "etching" illustrated above. Price 2s. 6d. (2s. 8d. including postage).

A Knitted Doll: Oddments of wool or yarn left from more "serious" knitting make these delightful toys, which stand about a foot high. Instructions for the Sailor in Good Housekeeping Knitting Bulletin No. 78, and for "Toni," the girl doll, in Bulletin No. 79, each price 6d. post free. Make them now for Christmas.

Department, 30 Grosvenor Gardens, London, S.W.1

Your Christm

USE colour boldly for your Christmas table this year. Try the effect of a scarlet table-covering with a centre-piece of tall white candles, and twin white cornucopias spilling out a collection of colourful fruit, evergreens and berries;

or—

A dark green table-cloth with a centrepiece of radiating sprays of fir cones and pine cones gilded, some touched with white paint. Set small scarlet candles at intervals round the table;

and—

You can add a lovely note of decoration to any table by placing small posies of evergreens tied with green or scarlet velvet ribbon at each place.

For the Dining-room sprays of whitened beech branches hung with small glass witch balls;

Cape gooseberries attached to tall branches;

A silver hoop with clusters of small pine cones and ribbons and holly berries hung round the table light;

A witch ball made from two small wooden hoops completely covered with brightly coloured velvet ribbon and hung with silver stars and bright toys;

Silver stars pasted on to cheap parchment lamp-shades;

A child's toy horse and cart filled with pine sprays, berries, miniature toys and frosted cotton-wool;

A small tree on a side-table in the dining-room with frosted leaves. (To frost them, wet the leaves and sprinkle thickly with Epsom salts);

Golden "angels" for the table-napkins—cut out from stiff adhesive paper, painted with gold paint;

Streamers made of a coloured cord suspending oranges, leaves, silver bells and blue-birds cut out from stiff coloured adhesive paper—two sides pasted together with the cord running between them.

as ... Table

By Christine Palmer

For Children's Parties concentrate on room decoration and keep the table as simple as possible.

Frosted cotton-wool laid along the window-sills, with large irregular pieces pressed flat up against the window, will give a "snowed-up" effect. Cotton-wool forms a good background, too, for little figures, gnomes, elves and village scenes which can be tucked nonchalantly into the "odd corners" which children love.

In other parts of the room arrange large sprays of long, bare branches and twigs, along the tops of which you can draw a brush dipped in white paint, to give the effect of snow lying heavily on them.

Candles—be as extravagant as you can with them, using all sizes, shapes and colours. If you can't get coloured candles, paint ordinary white ones with bands of colour, stars, hearts and crescent moons. Be sure to put candles in holders of some kind and don't place them too near cotton-wool. And take care that all candles are put out when the room is left.

EVERY family their own book publishers—this Christmas when rag-books are unobtainable. We suggest the young artist members of the family work out the designs as simply as possible and in whatever colour schemes the rag-bag materials suggest. Then the needleworkers take over and stitch the pieces in place, adding details, such as eyes, etc., with coloured threads. Next the bookbinders bind the pages together and "publish" in time to find a place on the family Christmas tree.

If the "pages" are of thick material (and every page can be a different colour), the designs are best worked in thin materials. But if you use thin materials for the pages, these should be doubled, as real rag-books used to be.

Try your ideas first with coloured paper pasted in a paper book (which, of course, is an alternative method of production).

We are sure children can think of lots more ideas than those suggested here and on the next page. Very simple, large designs are the easiest to sew in place.

Illustrated by Tage Werner

The WANTED BABIES that

By Len Chaloner

WHATEVER may be the findings or policies of the Royal Commission set up to study our population problems, it has already brought home to most people the fact that these are not just mathematical calculations about a remote world a hundred or so years hence, but that they are current and immensely human and personal problems, the effects of which are already being felt in our community. Even to-day, compared with twenty-five years ago, we have a greater proportion of elderly—pensionable—people to young, productive ones, and this proportion must increase side by side with the gradual decrease in the actual numbers of our population.

Mr. Carr Saunders, a member of the Royal Commission and Chairman of the Population Investigation Committee, a body that has been studying population trends for a considerable period, put the matter into a nutshell when he observed that we must first discover *how* fertility is falling, so that from this we may be in a better position to discover *why* fertility is falling.

On one aspect of this question of *how* fertility is falling, medical evidence is already able to give us evidence that will undoubtedly receive the most serious and sympathetic consideration of the Commission. It is, moreover, in a direction that hitherto has not been very generally recognised.

Where married people have no family, it has generally been assumed that the choice is a deliberate one. Medical opinion has gone forward recently with the view that this is by no means always the case*—that many, in fact, to whom no babies arrive would like to have them. It is natural, of course, that they do not broadcast such personal disappointment among their friends, and even conceal this private sorrow under the assumption that they do not really want a family. The wife, particularly, has always suffered from the idea that, when wanted babies are not forthcoming, the sterility is hers alone. Incorrect as modern medicine has found this to be (sterility being quite as likely to rest with the husband as with the wife), this old idea has often greatly increased the burdens of a woman who has already felt keenly the disappointment and frustration of her maternal instincts.

But medicine to-day has not only discovered that infertility may lie with either partner. It has learned how to help such conditions much more than formerly. Moreover, though some cases may require operation, others may simply require injections, or hormone substances taken by the mouth. The difficulty is that hospital staffs are heavily depleted, and specialised knowledge is usually needed to diagnose and advise such cases, while the treatment is liable to be expensive.

It is with all this in mind that the British Social

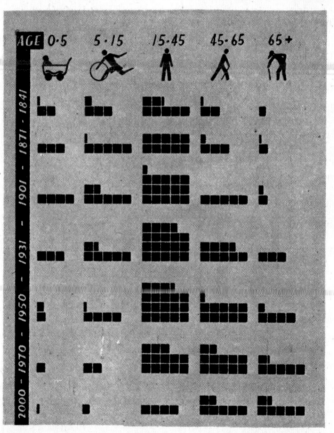

Each square in the diagram represents one million people. The figures for the populations in 1950, 1970 and 2000 are based on an estimate which assumes that recent trends in birth- and death-rates will continue in the future

(Reproduced by permission of Messrs. Secker & Warburg, from "Parents Revolt," by Richard and Kathleen Titmuss.)

* *Why don't the Wanted Babies always Come?* British Social Hygiene Council.

STAY AWAY

MOTHERS' ENQUIRY SERVICE: The Good Housekeeping Children's Doctor answers by letter questions on mothers' and children's general health, diet, etc., and a selection of letters is published in the magazine. Replies cannot be sent by return. The Doctor cannot, of course, deal with queries on the treatment or diagnosis of disease, which must be referred to your own doctor, nor does she answer questions not concerned with mothers and children. Address your letters to the Children's Doctor, c/o Good Housekeeping, 28-30 Grosvenor Gardens, London, S.W.1, and please remember to enclose a stamped addressed envelope for her reply by post.

Hygiene Council is sponsoring an effort to establish in London a special clinic for advising the partners of infertile marriages, enabling *both* partners to be examined by specialists with knowledge of various aspects of infertility. The Fertility Clinic would be open to all patients, to general practitioners, hospitals and other institutions wishing to make use of its services, and it would supply treatment, or guide the treatment given by the patient's own doctor.

It is estimated that £5,000 will be needed before the Clinic can be equipped and founded, but it is believed that by charging fees on a sliding scale to those who could afford them, it would become self-supporting in a short time. If the first Clinic becomes successfully established, it is hoped that others will follow.

Though Fertility Clinics are new in this country, they have been tried out in America, in Sweden and in Germany, where in the last two instances they were part of a wider policy. This proposed London Clinic is not, however, an official measure or connected with the work of the Royal Commission.

Just why there should be this high incidence of infertility in modern times is not yet clear. How far, for instance, may it be attributed to the later marriages dictated by present-day economic factors, or to the conditions of urban or industrial life?

In considering our own problems of population, it has to be borne in mind that we are by no means alone in these difficulties.

Various means were adopted in France, Sweden, Italy and Germany to increase their populations, but the problem remained elusive in spite of marriage loans, fertility clinics and children's allowances. After the War the question will undoubtedly become even more pressing. It requires little imagination to appreciate that populations write to-morrow's history and frame its geography in the process. In a world centring so much upon industrialisation, these fundamental things had been long overlooked or undervalued, and motherhood had been long the Cinderella of vocations. War, however, has shown in unexpected ways the vital rôle of the family.

In the final paragraph of a research pamphlet, *Population and Fertility*, written by Drs. D. V. Glass and C. P. Blacker, and published by the (Continued on page 102)

THE GOOD HOUSEKEEPING CHILDREN'S DOCTOR ADVISES:

My daughter is now 4½ months old, and is a happy, contented, intelligent baby, giving no trouble at home. Until she was three months old she would go to anyone, and then, whilst at my husband's home, the dog barked most ferociously, close to her, and frightened her so much she wouldn't be comforted. Since then she will not go to strangers without much coaxing, and seems frightened when I take her to a strange house. This is especially so when I visit my husband's home, and she does seemed frightened of the dog, who is allowed to run round and barks a lot. In between visits she seems to improve. The attitude taken is that she is a baby who will just not go to people, that she will grow out of it, and must get used to the dog; but I do think it is fright, as she will lie in her pram, where she feels safe, and "talk" to perfect strangers. I would discontinue visits, but my husband is overseas, and I am living with my people, so the situation is not easy. Can you suggest the best course to adopt?

She is a contented baby, and sleeps all night, but weighs only 13 lb. 5 oz.; at birth she was 8 lb. 12 oz., and I think she ought to be heavier now; I am breast-feeding her. She is well covered, and firm, though not fat.

It is always difficult trying to bring up a baby in someone else's house, though you are not actually living with your husband's people, and I can understand that they might easily become rather jealous if you discontinued your visits, and yet continued to live with your own people.

Nevertheless, a sudden loud noise certainly does upset a young baby, and I think your only course is to ask them to come to your house and leave the dog at home. Also you should state quite firmly that you cannot come to their house with baby until they understand that the dog must be kept away from baby, and under proper control.

Later baby will like him much better, but at the moment he is nothing but a loud noise to her, and that is very frightening.

I agree that her gain in weight might be rather more rapid, and suggest that she has a small feed consisting of milk 2½ oz., water 1 oz., patent barley preparation 1 level teaspoon and sugar 1 teaspoon. Make it as you would a sauce, and give from a cup and spoon before the 10 a.m., and possibly the 6 p.m., breast feed.

By Marion Henderson

Illustrated

by

C. F. Tunnicliffe

Flowers of the

WE are a nation of flower-lovers, even if our gardens now wear their "battle-dress." In the very darkest days of the war, when the familiar face of our everyday existence had grown sinister, we persisted in growing a few flowers and cutting the very reduced lawns left to us from the vegetable patches. Dorothy Thompson, on her first war-time visit to this country, expressed surprise and pleasure at the bright clumps of marigolds and the neatly shorn grass in the Temple Gardens, London. It was characteristic of the British nation, she thought, that they continued to grow flowers while fear and danger were so near.

We who stayed at home in those days held fast to beauty, because we believed that she was the "most certain solace for so many human sorrows." Our men and women in the Forces did the same, when they went abroad hugging precious memories of the wild and cultivated flowers that grow in their own countryside. To them the garden at home has always remained a sanctuary of flowers, with trees, shrubs and bushes, rockery and lawn—a place where they walked in the days of peace, and enjoyed the colour and fragrance of their favourite roses.

For them the spiritual essence found in flowers brought compensation for the loss of so much they held dear, and so

their letters home began to contain more than a passing reference to the blooms they found growing on the fighting fronts across the seas. I have beside me several letters sent by a soldier in North Africa, who, though he has been two years in that country, has never grown accustomed to the sudden miracle of colour that transforms the arid wastes of brown and grey so early in the year. He has sent me several zinc-topped boxes containing lemons and oranges, from the orchards whose bloom is a feast of colour at a time when we at home are hopefully looking for the first crocus.

His very first letter, written shortly before Christmas, describes the glory of the purple-flowering bougainvillea he found growing on a farm in Tunisia. "I never saw such colour," he wrote, "perhaps because at this moment there is a gorgeous-hued hoopoe pecking for grubs under the purple tree, and I cannot make up my mind whether the bird's orange and blue and rich brown outmatch the beauty of the bougainvillea."

He described the multitude of annuals and bulbs which grow in North Africa, especially the small, white narcissi he found growing wild everywhere. As for the cyclamen and tulips on the battlefields of Kasserine, they were—to quote from his letter—"more like the colours on a stage than anything else." He described, too, the cedar forests that crest

Fighting Fronts

the mountains south of Algiers—it was in a cedar wood he came across a particularly lovely tulip with rich orange petals, growing up through a wild carpet of yellow flowers which looked like helianthemum.

Gladioli grow wild in North Africa, and they seem to be in one shade—a purplish pink—with blossoms smaller than those we used to grow for exhibition purposes in pre-war days. The bulbs grow profusely in the orchards, the vineyards, the woods and the fields, and close beside them white daisies make a "milky way" with their bloom.

Of the oleanders which belong to that fighting front, my soldier-friend writes: "I never met those lovely shrubs before, except in books, especially in poetry books. But here they are found beside every little stream, as common as the wild kingcups at home. Oleanders growing out of the sand or shingle, wherever there is a trickle of water, and every shrub covered over with masses of clear pink blossoms—some are double, others single, and invariably the single-petalled flowers give more perfume."

Those exotic flowers remind our men in North Africa that the earth goes on renewing herself despite man's frightfulness to man. They also help to keep fresh the pictures of our own green countryside, where the bloom, though it be sparse compared with that of other lands, is infinitely more precious to those who can only see it with the "inward eye" which is the bliss of separation as it is of solitude. Of the wild poppies that always follow battlefields, and which abound in North Africa, my friend writes: "Here they grow in blocks of scarlet, great blooms, rather like the Shirley poppies I used to grow in our garden at home, with double petals, and so different from those tiny wildings that grow among the corn in the little farms of the Highlands of Scotland." The last letter I received contained a reference to the heather found on that fighting front: "Picture great patches of white heather," writes the soldier, "growing along the edge of a pine forest in this part of the world! It made me home-sick to look at it, for I thought of the quilts of purple heather in my (Continued on page 46)

Dual-

THESE days, all our rooms have a dual-purpose look. We have been billeted or billeted-upon; we exist in halves of houses or the smallest flats; we have neither the help to run large homes nor the time to do it ourselves. Bedroom-study, living-room-nursery: these are livable combinations, and can be made quite pleasant ones, although all rooms present some problem in conversion and must be arranged to suit the basic features—windows, heating appliances and available wall space.

The bedroom-study shown here has been planned to look as much of a study and as little of a bedroom as possible. In circumstances like these, a divan is preferable to a bed. The bedding is tidily and hygienically stored either in a lidded box at one end of the bed, or else in a "sack" of network hanging in a specially ventilated part of the cupboard. The "sack" hangs on four hooks, with the front opening when the two front hooks are undone. A wash-basin, with dressing-table accoutrements, is usefully fitted into part of the big recessed cupboard.

Personality Rooms

Plans and arrangements designed by Ernst L. Freud, M.Inst.R.A.

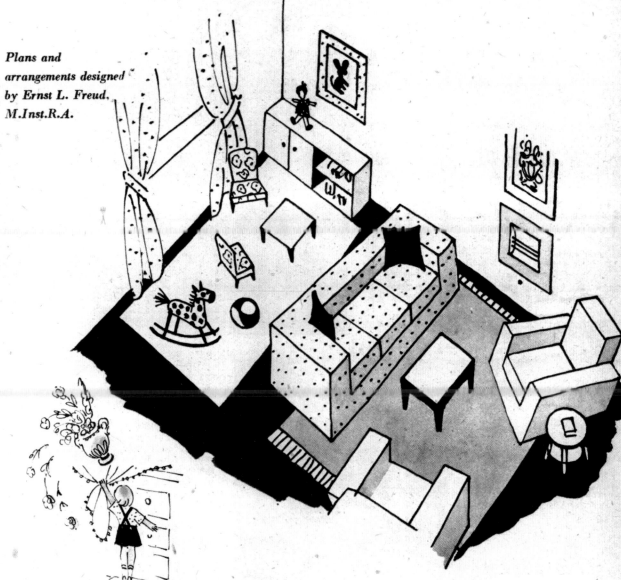

LIVING-ROOM-NURSERY: this combination needs some care. The baby must be protected from dangers arising out of the room, and the room must certainly be protected from the baby.

Best plan is to divide the room, so far as practicable, into two. One way to do this is to group the heavy furniture round the fireplace, and to clear another part of the room for junior play. A washable rug should be set down here, over the existing carpet if necessary, and the baby's own things—small-scale furniture, toy-cupboard and shelves—arranged on it. A wise mother will remove precious breakables from every part of the room and protect delicate chair-coverings, cushions or tapestries.

WOMAN'S Road to FREEDOM —

I SMILED derisively.

On my desk, from under a welter of Press cuttings from America, protruded a large paragraph—"Cook by Television!" Manufacturers, it seemed, were promising post-war sets that would enable the housewife to watch the joint in the kitchen-oven while sitting sewing in the living-room.

One more silly gadget for a few more silly women!

Or one more step to freedom?

Which?

From time to time, articles and books are published, lectures are held, protests are made, all more or less directly concerned with the emancipation of women. No homage can be too great for such as Emily Davies and Josephine Butler, Sophia Jex Blake and Elizabeth Garrett Anderson; no gratitude too fulsome for those who helped to break down the most flagrant legal injustices which regarded woman as a dependent and a chattel, and helped to bring about the Married Woman's Property Act, the Enabling Bill, the Woman's Disabilities Bill, and women's suffrage. But no struggle, however determined and courageous, could have been waged, no victory, except a worthless and theoretical one, could have been won, without the aid of a less publicised, less articulate rebellion—women's struggle against domestic slavery.

Yes, for all the magnificent triumphs, it looked as if women—Britons though they might be—for ever, ever, ever would be slaves—to one simple fact: the human race had to be fed and clothed. It is true that civilisation had developed far from the age when man found the food and woman cooked it. Very few men, indeed, had to find the food, but most women still had to cook it—or superintend the cooking. Woman's rôle, though more complex, more refined, remained in essence unalterable—her emblems a needle, a broom, a fire. It was all very well for a handful of women, for the most part unmarried, to break away from such ties, but unless we belonged to their somewhat too-exclusive company, or were pampered members of the nobility, or—yet more unlikely—left our goose-feather beds to go exploring with the wraggle-taggle gipsies; apart from these and one or two

The sewing machine . . . gas and electric stoves and other

rôle they have played in freeing

by MACHINE

By Marjorie Hessell Tiltman

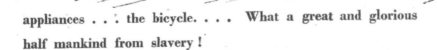

other minor exceptions, we ordinary women must remain in bondage to those three taskmasters. Pleasant our lot may have been made by family love, comfortable by the service of other women, enjoyable by prosperity—it was yet slavery, because there was no escaping from it.

So at any rate our mothers believed; or our grandmothers, if we are twenty and not forty.

Providence, however, has a way of providing solutions as the need arises—when we ask, and when we *do*. Though often we grasp them without realising it. The social revolution which is still in progress has been fought with a very definite weapon—the weapon of machinery. To associate women, rather than men, with machinery, may at first hearing sound peculiar, but I want to reinforce my suggestion by a quotation from a book by a young American called *Beyond the Urals*. John Scott went out to Russia in 1931, he worked for five years as an engineer in Magnitogorsk, and gives one of the most balanced, detached and intelligent analyses I have ever read of Russia's industrialisation, and I was in Russia in 1930— and in Stalingrad for the opening of the greatest tractor factory in the world! From it I quote a picture of a typical girl operative in the rolling mills:

"Shura was an operator. . . . She had under her control a ten-thousand-horse-power direct-current motor . . . and a score of auxiliary motors of various kinds. . . . She was a village girl who had been very sick, which had been the cause of her taking the operators' course instead of doing more active work. . . . She understood the electrical controls which she operated, and while her knowledge of theoretical physics was not extensive, she knew enough to be a thoroughly competent operator. Beyond this it was a question of a simple mechanical and nervous dexterity, and at this she was a master. . . . In many jobs, such as crane-operating, mill-operating, and so forth, where reliability, dexterity and consistency were required rather than physical strength, women largely replaced men in Magnitogorsk. . . . Their only disadvantage was that, with a birth-rate in 1937 of thirty-three to one thousand, they were prone to be running away for maternity vacations too frequently, and losing the knack of their work."

Well, that is to-day, and because few of us are old enough to have witnessed the beginnings of the revolution, we are inclined to take it for granted. Let me recall one of the most famous indictments ever written on behalf of women—Thomas Hood's " Song of the Shirt " : (*Continued on page* **102**)

appliances . . . the bicycle. . . . What a great and glorious

half mankind from slavery !

AMONG letters which still reach me about "Nobody's Children," in the December issue of GOOD HOUSEKEEPING, are a number on the subject of full legal adoption.

Some parents write to tell of their happiness with adopted children, whom they appear to have found with little difficulty, and to say that they consider adoption the best thing for homeless children. I could not agree with them more enthusiastically: I would urge adoption for all except a very few.

Typical is this extract from an Essex reader's letter: "My husband and I adopted two babies, a boy now nearly six and a girl now three. Delightful youngsters they are (though sometimes little devils!). My feeling is that the best solution is adoption. More should be known about the proceedings—the patient help of the Society that finds the baby, the sympathy and untiring assist-

in vain for a child. There are several reasons. First, there is an overwhelming demand for girl babies. People believe they will get more comfort out of a girl. She will come straight home from school and bring her little friends with her, while a boy may spend all his waking hours on sports, clubs and other outside activities. The demand for girls is so steady and consistent that it creates a shortage of girls, while boys are left unadopted.

Second, a mother has a right, quite naturally, to give away her baby herself, without any legal or other restrictions. The average mother would rather die than part for ever with her child, but women with illegitimate babies are often driven to do it. What else can the poor girl do, especially if her family does not know about the baby or has "disowned" her because of it? In this way

LOUISE MORGAN'S promised

ADOP

Another aspect of that vital problem

ance of the magistrates who hear applications for adoption orders. More should be known, too, about the new adoption laws. Some people fear adoption may be too expensive. It cost me exactly 17s. 6d."

But here is a very different story, from a Hampshire reader, and representing a far greater number of letters: "We are a couple who wish to adopt one of the 150,000 children you wrote about, but this appears to be an impossibility. We have tried three registered adoption societies, many nurseries, the County gynæcologist, the County N.S.P.C.C. officer, and others—all in vain. We have a boy of our own of four and half. A second boy died, and there is no hope of our having more. We want a girl, and if possible, two others later, a boy and a girl. We are not sick. We have two houses, one in the country. Our boy will go to prep. school and Winchester, and the girl would have a similar education. I love children and before my marriage taught P.T."

It seems incredible that such a family, where a "nobody's nothing" would have a chance of sharing all the good things of life, has to ask

many babies find their way into a kind of black market when they are only ten days or a fortnight old.

Third, there is a flaw in the new Adoption Act which came into operation in 1943. This Act was intended to raise adoption to a higher plane than handing a baby over the counter like a package of tea, but in actual practice it allows many of the old evil customs to remain. Under the "third party" clause anybody, whoever he or she may be, may introduce a child to parents who wish to adopt one, so long as the fact is reported to the local health or welfare authority. The authority then visits the parents' home, the application is made to the court, and the whole business is concluded, signed and sealed in three or four weeks. No probationary period, during which the new relationship can be tried out to see if it is harmonious, is required. By sheer luck "third party" adoption may turn out a happy arrangement, but the chances are that the adopter and child may be temperamentally opposed—when only misery for both will result.

Modern research strongly condemns this kind

Photograph by courtesy of the National Children Adoption Association (Incorp.)

of adoption, especially in present circumstances, when authorities are so overworked that they can make only cursory visits and investigations. Moreover, having nowhere to put the baby, they are tempted to seize on any home. What can be learned in a couple of weeks about the baby's or the parents' history? How can it be decided in a brief visit or two whether the child will be happy in this particular home? Is it fair to dispose of the child's life, perhaps seventy-five years of it, in less than a month?

The truth is that adoption, and indeed, child-care in general, in this country is on a deplorably low plane. We do not regard the child as a human being in his own right. Adoption is not regarded from *his* point of view, though it is his life which is at stake. No, adoption is regarded rather as a method of solution for some adult's problem. The first thing we have to do is to pull

approached by a dubious person who offers to take the baby and give it a "good home." Ill, worried, exhausted by her experiences, in too low a state of mind to cope with her difficulties, she is only too easily persuaded, especially when a money present is offered, no questions asked, and no forms given her to fill. Recently one baby girl given up by her mother changed hands three times in as many weeks, money being passed each time. The baby ended in hospital with a serious disease.

This could be stopped at once if there were convalescent hostels where the mothers could stay until they got back their strength, gave the baby a good start, found work where they could keep the baby themselves, or arranged for a proper adoption. Hostels of this type should be a part of every maternity hospital scheme as an essential service. They would wipe out a type of shady

article on

TION

—the future of our children

ourselves up to the new plane on which we view adoption solely and wholly as the child's problem.

What is best for the child? That is our touchstone. And incidentally, by finding what is best for the child, we automatically help the real mother and ensure the happiness of the adoptive parents.

To return to the first point, it would ease the situation enormously if people would not insist on having girls. I have never understood this preference, and I am convinced it is not on a sound basis. More depends on the individual than on the sex, and there are many boys who have just as deep ties with their parents and home as any girl. Remember that the essential thing is not whether the child is a girl or boy, but whether it is the kind of individual who would be happy in your home and would make you happy as well.

What can be done to stop unmarried mothers giving their babies away just after they leave hospital or maternity home? The situation to-day is a disgrace to the country. The mother is often

maternity home where unmarried mothers are charged large fees which actually are adoption fees, because the understanding is that the home will make all arrangements for adoption, thus "saving face" for the mother.

Finally, the "third party" clause of the Adoption Act should be amended. A probationary period of three or four months should be made necessary before the adoption is made legal. Also no untrained, inexperienced or unqualified persons should be allowed to introduce a baby to an adoptive mother, not even if they are doctors, almoners or magistrates.

Mrs. D. C. Plummer, who as secretary of the National Children Adoption Association (Incorp.), has in the past twenty years arranged well over six thousand successful adoptions, and who knows as much as, if not more than, any person in the country about the subject, made this challenging comment: "In the last June quarter, 13,687 illegitimate babies were born. Only a very small percentage of the girls reached us. What became of the others?"

The only sound way (Continued on page 51)

These men need

Back Room COOKS

The job of repairing Southern England's bomb-damaged houses is a tremendous one. The men, who come mostly from the provinces, are doing heavy and dangerous work—when these pictures were taken V-bombs were still falling around them. They need somewhere to sleep, food to eat. This is the story of just one of the sixty-eight Special Repair Service camps in the devastated area. Below, a few of the S.R.S. cooks taking a cookery lesson in Good Housekeeping Institute. The lecturer reports that she has rarely had a more enthusiastic and keenly intelligent audience

Back view of

good food and plenty of it

In ten minutes' time they will be mending homes again

SOMEWHERE in Southern England, two cooks are serving up four meals a day, seven days a week, to fifty hungry men. The fifty men are working to repair bombed houses; they live and eat in huts specially built for them in the middle of the devastation they work on. The two cooks are working no less hard or gallantly, in fact rather more so, because they are not really cooks at all. They are bricklayers.

"They just couldn't find any cooks for the job when we came down here, so I said I'd have a shot," says big Joe in his slow, broad North Country accent, and "Well, it's as good a job as any other," chimes in little Bob. "I was brought up with six sisters, so I reckon I know a bit about cooking. We get on fine."

Their kitchen is no chromium-plated, press-button dream. It has a concrete floor, one small sink, a big coal range and two cauldrons in which they keep water simmering. Two small hatches connect it with the men's dining-room, and a larder cuts off one corner. The saucepans and baking-tins are enormous, as you would suppose, but the only other piece of modern equipment in sight is a potato-peeling machine.

"We get up at five," says Joe. "Have to. First there's the fires to
(Continued on page 98)

Two hundred meals a day need good timing

Nothing palatial here, but they are cheerful about discomforts

a skilled operation

4 WAYS TO

Go Windswept and Fluffy

At seventeen you can get away with a carelessly combed mane tossed back over your shoulders ; you can even look glamorous with your hair blown all hither and thither as you come in from feeding the fowls. Over thirty, no.

You need a little more sophistication and a lot more satin sleekness. Choose your hair-style carefully—an easily managed style for preference, so that you can keep it always at peak of perfection yourself. Learn to be clever about pinning up at night. Treasure your hairpins and hair grips, cherish that fine hair net and wear it every night, whether you've pinned up or not. Experiment with scarves to keep your curls protected from blustery weather and sudden rain. There's bound to be one kind of scarf-turban that suits you ; when you've found it you can keep a scarf in your pocket and be proof against the worst the weather can do.

*Illustrations
by
Tage
Werner*

Throw a Temperament a Day

Tantrums have a dual effect. They keep your mind juvenile, they make your complexion old. They cause frown lines and little tight creases at the corners of your mouth ; they put an edge on your voice and a hardness in your eyes. . . .

If you'd stay young . . . cultivate serenity. The calm outlook, the masculine why-worry air, is the one to adopt. Life won't be any easier if you fuss and fume, and you'll certainly be less charming to see and know. So next time you find yourself ready to breathe fire—take a deep breath instead. Unclench your hands, count ten silently. Then put on your prettiest smile and ask *nicely* for what you want.

LOOK YOUR AGE

Let Your Weight Settle on Your Hip-bones

The middle-aged spread is always below the waist, you notice. There's a middle-aged walk, too—a walk that is perilously near a plod. It all comes of letting the world and its worries get you down. You walk along concentrating on the children's supper; and gradually the food problem weights your shoulders, depresses your waistline, makes your feet as heavy as lead.

Rise above the food problem; children need meals, but they also need an attractive mother. Lift up that surplus weight from the region of your hip-bones, put it back where it belongs. Hold yourself as tall as you can —not rigidly, but as if you were trying to get nearer the sun. Keep your shoulders back, your waist tucked in and your feet pointing straight ahead, and your posture will already be infinitely better. And "walk light"— you can do it, quite consciously, whatever your weight may be. Remember, when you get home, not to slouch or slump in your chair. You should be able to let yourself down into a chair gracefully, easily, slowly; and if you can't, it's a clear case for a gentle daily dozen, with more bending-from-the-waist movements, and a regular daily walk.

Neglect Your Hands

" Show me a woman's hands and I'll tell you her age," said a famous man, and though war-work has been harder on our hands than on any other feature, there are still many unnecessarily old-looking pairs about. The easiest possible way to neglect your hands is to think that they are so bad they are not worth bothering about.

Even the most " hopeless " hands can be revived beyond imagination by just a little care. A face pack, bought from the chemist and thickly plastered on; a twice-daily rub with an emollient tablet; a course of creaming-and-sleeping-in-gloves (old cotton gloves for preference); and a good manicure, will take ten years off your fingertips in as many days.

By
Muriel Cox

National Scourge

By Louise Morgan

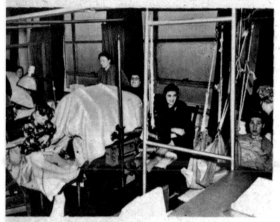

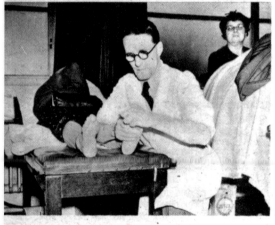

From top to bottom : A new patient is questioned for his social history ; patients receiving a variety of treatments ; a skilful blind masseur ; paraffin-wax treatment, which is helpful for some conditions

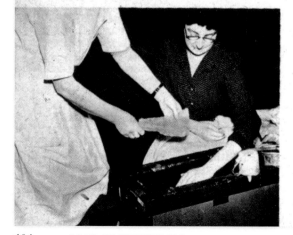

DR. A, the great specialist from the West End, sits in the tiny office of the Rheumatism Unit at St. Stephen's London County Council General Hospital in the Fulham Road, Chelsea. Dr. A is one of the specialists attached to the Rheumatism Unit.

He is a big, calm, smiling man, swathed in dazzling white, and the tired and worried faces of patients as they hobble in one by one or are pushed in on stretchers or wheeled chairs light up as soon as they see that smile, like grim landscapes suddenly drenched in sunshine.

This crowded little room is a treatment in itself. There is Dr. A's smile, and the warmth of his greeting, as if each patient were his one and only. There is the bustling, merry little hospital Sister, who somehow contrives to hand him immediately all he asks for, as if she kept a cupboard in the air. There is the masseuse and the staff nurse, both on their toes, and with their eyes wide open. There is the house doctor, who likes a joke, and a serious young American woman doctor who, by acting as a locum tenens for the medical registrar absent on leave, is giving the hospital a spell of help and widening her own clinical experience at the same time.

In and out pass others of this remarkable rheumatism team as they are needed—the almoner, dietetist, occupational therapist and radiologist or X-ray expert. A patient here can have the help of a dozen different specialists, including orthopædic surgeon, pathologist and dentist, each contributing to the study and mastery of his case. He goes out re-armed for the battle with the dread enemy which has invaded his system.

In comes an unusually tall, slender and pretty girl in the uniform of the A.T.S., sent by her medical officer as a suspected case of early rheumatoid arthritis. She looks too young and lovely, too much alive, to be marked down by such a horrible disease. In a seemingly casual way which conceals the swift and sure technique of the master, Dr. A gives her a once-over.

" Touch your toes. Bend backwards. Raise your arms. Grip my hand. Good."

He examines the X-ray photographs of her hands and lungs which the hospital Sister fixes on the lighted glass screen on his table and reads the report of the blood tests. Then he dictates his verdict, which the medical registrar takes down.

" We'd better write the M.O. We consider it is *not* early rheumatoid arthritis. It is purely a peripheral, vascular disturbance," and he adds technical details of treatment.

Everybody in the room breathes a sigh of relief, and the A.T.S. girl beams. She is more than pretty ; she is positively beautiful. Dr. A gets up and shakes her hand. " You can continue with your duties," he says. " Meantime we'll build you up and improve your circulation. You ought to be better in six weeks' time. Come to see me then."

No.1—Rheumatism

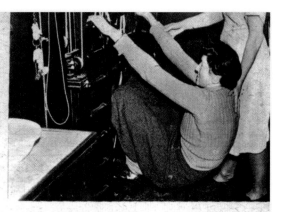

Photographs Sport & General

From top to bottom : *One of many forms of gymnastic treatment ; mechanical means of helping movements and exercises ; forms of electrical treatment ; the interview with the dietetist, which may be all-important*

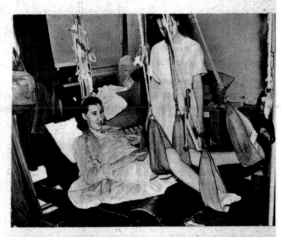

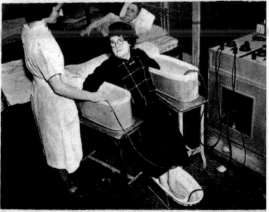

" Oh, thank you, doctor," she says in a glowing voice, and the next person comes in.

Dr. A has just time to comment, " They catch these cases early in the Forces now—a great thing," before he shakes hands with a man who walks as if his body were a rigid box. This man is an advanced case of *spondylitis deformans* or " poker back." But he grins cheerfully.

" It's the best winter I've had in fifteen years, doctor," he says. " The breathing exercises you gave me and the postural exercises have benefited me enormously." Dr. A checks him over, varies his treatment slightly, and after he goes tells the group that he is doing a full-time job as blast-furnace worker in a war factory, and is an outstanding example of what a 100 per cent. co-operative patient can do even with one of the most crippling and depressing forms of rheumatism.

An undersized, bespectacled schoolgirl comes in with a please-excuse-me-for-living air. In a light, vague voice she says " pains all over " keep her awake at night. Her coat is thin, her underclothes scanty and very grubby. Dr. A examines her carefully and tenderly, chatting with her all the time, drawing her out. When she goes, with a pinch more faith in herself than when she entered, he says, " This is a case for the almoner. Please ask her to visit the home, do a survey and let me have it. The psychological aspect, diet, clothes, housing—all these things are factors here. It is nonsense to think there is one cure for rheumatism. Each case is different from any other, and requires different treatment. One must get the whole picture of each individual in his work and in his home."

A little nurse who has come from a neighbouring hospital with fibrositis in arm and side is in time to hear and admire this bit of medical exposition.

" How do you feel ? " he asks her.

" Slightly uncomfortable in the costal region," she replies briskly.

He laughs. " Let's have a look at it." She has done a professional job of getting ready for him, and in one nip is ready. Off comes her neat coat, and there she stands in pretty, pink silk tailored brassière and panties, her stockings in a neat roll above her ankles. He decides to give her an injection. Sister holds her shoulders comfortably and says, " Take a deep breath, nurse." The little nurse does not even wince as the needle discharges a full load into her muscles.

Dr. A goes on talking. " The trouble with you is over-work, and doing the kind of work you were never built for, on top of your own. There should be more cleaners and pantry-maids in hospitals."

For four hours on end he carries on, without a break even for a cup of coffee. They keep coming in—a Viennese pianist whose gaunt frame seems to huddle round his pain-ridden left hand as if in protection, a waiter (*Continued on page* 104)

Entertaining à la

HOSPITALITY, like every other art, needs plenty of practice and means taking infinite trouble.

Good hostesses now spare themselves less than ever before—they search the shops and markets for good things to eat, carry home large baskets of fresh vegetables from a country visit or from a distant but reliable greengrocer, and never miss a new idea for cooking or serving food.

Vision and foresight were never more necessary for entertaining. The pound or two of sugar spared now to make a little red-currant jelly helps to serve mutton or hare with more distinction in the winter; a pot of chives grown and watered carefully on a London window-sill or balcony means added piquancy and a note of colour in sauces and garnishes. And why don't more people in town or country plant their own bay tree? A bay tree will flour-

ish in a tub by the kitchen door or in the garden, and the flavour of a freshly-picked bay leaf is so much better than that of a dried one.

Bottles of Apple Purée, conserved when apples are plentiful, give a basis for many good sweets when fruit is scarce, and can be used for cold Apple Sauce with thin slices of cold pork or hot Apple Sauce with Fried Spiced Ham.

All kinds of bottled fruits are valuable for winter entertaining, but pears are particularly good for quick dinner-party sweets : served very cold with hot chocolate sauce or with a little crab-apple jelly and grated chocolate, or with Melba Sauce, they form an excellent " made-in-five-minutes " sweet.

Home-bottled tomatoes, tomato juice and a few good chutneys and sauces will prove useful as cooking ingredients for savoury dishes.

Golden Rules for Parties

Having decided on the kind of party, chosen the menu and invited your guests, concentrate on the setting and remember that at even the most informal party an attractive background and smooth service are of first importance. Limitations of supplies will deter no enterprising hostess, and post-war parties will be both gay and chic in spite of the difficulties. When you give a party a few good rules to follow are :

- Never undertake more than you can do with ease —the pleasure of your guests will be spoilt if you are tired at the party. It is most important that you should be serene and calm and ready to give your full attention to your visitors.

- Don't exceed your budget. Remember that what suits your surroundings is in good taste; that beauty need not be costly and adds enormously even to the simplest affair, and that the foods served and the way you serve them are of equal importance. It is much better to give simple parties often, than to give one so expensively that you have to cut down on other entertaining.

- Rearrange your furniture, where necessary, to ensure that chairs, tables and lights are comfortably placed for your guests.

- Plan your parties to the minutest detail in advance and carry out your plans to the letter. If you must make unexpected or last-minute changes, be sure that they are in harmony with the original plans and that nothing has been forgotten.

- Choose guests who are congenial to each other and spare no effort to set them at ease and make them appear at their best.

Mode

By
**Christine
Palmer**

*(Combined Domestic
Subjects Diploma,
Leicester)*

Large Parties. Although dinner parties are the most gracious way of entertaining, staff and food problems now set a limit to the number of guests for formal entertaining of this kind.

The simplest way of entertaining a large number of people inexpensively is by giving tea or buffet parties.

Tea Parties. There is a pleasant leisured atmosphere at tea-time which lends itself to good conversation, and this can be a most elegant meal. A low table is helpful to the hostess for serving tea, and it is well worth while to give some thought to the comfortable placing of chairs and tables for your tea parties.

Serve good-quality China tea or Indian tea, and be sure that it is really well made and served hot and fresh throughout the party.

Get a reputation for the quality of the foods you serve for tea—for very good scones and varied breads, unusual home-made jams, delicately flavoured honeys and good sandwich-spreads. Find really good recipes for a few substantial cakes—a good Luncheon cake, Madeira cake, Seed cake, Gingerbread and Victoria Sandwich. Vary these occasionally with more unusual cakes or ice the plain mixtures and use good and varied fillings.

Buffet Parties are less taxing to the resources of a small household than formal meals, as most of the food can be prepared in advance and it does not matter if several types of china or silver make their appearance together. Parties of this kind permit of very flexible arrangements, and give you an opportunity to create charming effects with unusual table appointments.

One hot dish gives added interest to the usual platters of cold meats and salads. Few people like an entirely cold meal even on the hottest night, and the bringing in of one piping-hot dish adds interest. A creamy fish pie with a potato crust, for instance, or vegetables au gratin, or hot chipolata sausages with mashed potato are suitable dishes which can be prepared in advance and very quickly served.

Garden Parties. Food for garden parties can, and should, be simple : fresh fruit drinks, sandwiches and cakes of the biscuit type are particularly suitable.

Sandwiches can be prepared early in the day, wrapped in damp muslin and chilled in the refrigerator. The appearance of all sandwiches is improved when they are served on leaves. Vine leaves, strawberry leaves or crisp lettuce leaves add a cool note of colour to an open-air table.

A new hair style is as exciting as a new hat—
and generally speaking far cheaper. In these days you
can wear your hair up, down, round, wavy,
curly, straight. The variety is enormous, the choice
is a test of your intelligent interest in making yourself
as pretty as possible. Study these sketches, decide on
the shape and lines of your head, and style your hair to—

Round face

FLATTER YOUR FACE

FIRST, the shape from the front. Yours is a round face? Then pile your curls high, with flat up-brushed wings above the temples. A long face? Minimise the length with a curled-under fringe, a page-boy roll circling and framing your cheeks. That difficult "egg" shape, wider across the jaw than the forehead? Build up width at the sides and top. Heart shape? You are fortunate—you can have a tumble of curls for its own sake, and if summer tempts you to tie them off your forehead with a narrow ribbon bow, you'll look more engagingly heart-shaped than ever.

Long face

By

Muriel Cox

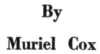

Egg-shaped

Heart-shaped

Large nose

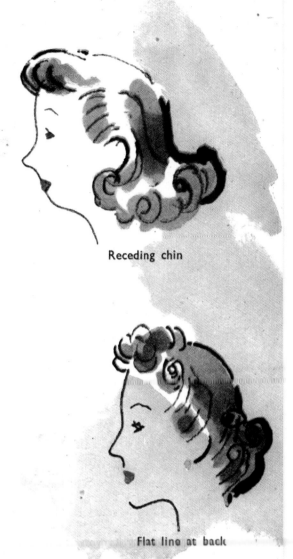

Receding chin

Flat line at back

A large nose needs some counter balancing weight, and a big bolster fringe is clever styling. The run-away chin demands a certain fluffiness and a generally youthful look; choose the loose bob that is popular around Hollywood again. A head flat at the back is easily camouflaged by back curls brushed slightly up. Incidentally, this is a very new line for almost all heads; it is smart, now, to show your hair-line at the back.

Lastly, three back views which explain themselves. The back of your head is seen nearly as often as the front, remember, and if you would look up-to-the-minute this summer the one thing you must *not* do is wear that easy, had-it-three-years, boring roll all around the back.

Long hair

Growing hair

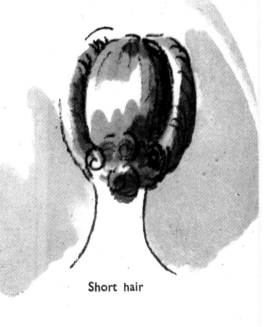

Short hair

NEW for EASTER

By Dilys Anthony
(*Combined Domestic Subjects Diploma,
Berridge House, London*)

Easter Biscuits

2 oz. margarine	A pinch of salt
2 oz. castor sugar	2 tablespoonfuls water
2 oz. plain flour	2 oz. currants
2 oz. self-raising flour	Almond essence

Cream the fat and sugar together until soft and white. Stir in the sieved flour and salt, and add the water, seeing that the mixture is just the right texture for rolling, if possible adding no extra liquid.

Divide the mixture in two, adding the fruit to one and the almond flavouring to the other. Roll out thinly, and cut the fruit mixture into rounds and the plain mixture into fancy shapes. Place on greased tins, and bake in a moderately hot oven (375° F.) for 10 to 15 minutes, until firm and a pale golden-brown colour. Cool on a rack.

To decorate, make a little chocolate icing by sieving together about 3 oz. of icing sugar and 1 oz. of cocoa. Add a few drops of water—sufficient to make the icing just leave a trail when poured from a spoon. Using a writing-pipe, and greaseproof paper bag, pipe birds or animals on the biscuits, or make nests out of the round ones by piping roughly round and round the edge of the biscuit to give a nest effect. Then make very tiny eggs of almond paste and fill the centre of the nest with them.

Almond Petal Cake

The basis of this recipe is our old friend ' Victoria Sandwich,' decorated with petals made from mock almond paste. If you want to have a real Simnel Cake, make a good fruit cake a week or so before Easter, top it with mock marzipan, and brown the marzipan under the grill.

3 oz. margarine	6 oz. self-raising flour
1 oz. cooking fat	About 4 tablespoonfuls
4 oz. castor sugar	water
2 eggs (fresh or dried)	Almond essence

Cream the fat and sugar together until soft and white. Beat in the eggs, a little at a time. Stir in the self-raising flour, keeping the mixture soft with the water. Add almond essence to flavour, and see that the mixture just drops from the spoon without shaking the spoon.

Turn into two greased sandwich tins. Bake in a moderately hot oven (375° F.) for about half an hour,

Try a new version of traditional dishes this year—biscuits in Easter dress, 'mock' Simnel Cake with almond-paste petals and, of course, hot-cross buns—made without eggs

until well risen and golden-brown, and until no impression is left on the cakes when a finger is placed on the top. Cool on a cake rack.

Fill with the following cream filling : Beat thoroughly 1 oz. margarine. Dissolve 1 oz. sugar in 1 tablespoonful of water, and beat into the margarine, a little at a time. Sieve in 2 tablespoonfuls of Household milk and sufficient almond essence to flavour.

For the petal top, make about ½ lb. of mock almond paste, using the recipe below. Roll it out very thinly on a sugared board, and cut out

Hot-cross Buns

½ lb. flour	¼ pint milk
¼ teaspoonful spice	2 oz. currants
½ teaspoonful salt	1 oz. margarine
½ oz. yeast	½ oz. shortcrust pastry for
1 oz. sugar	crosses, if liked

Sieve the flour, spice and salt into a bowl. Cream the yeast with one teaspoonful of the sugar and stir in the tepid milk. Add the remainder of the sugar, dried fruit and melted margarine to the flour. Mix in the creamed yeast with the hand, and beat well—a sticky dough should result. Add a little more

Children — and others — will make short work of 'birds'-nest' biscuits and chocolate shapes

Mock Simnel Cake can be made at the last minute as it is a sponge and has no fruit

rounds about 1 in. in diameter. Brush the top of the cake with jam, and arrange the petals, overlapping all over the top. We felt energetic, so we put them all round the sides as well. A little melted chocolate poured into the centre top of the cake gives an attractive finish.

Marzipan

3 oz. margarine	4 oz. sugar
¼ gill water	Few drops almond essence
	6 oz. soya flour

Put the margarine, water and sugar into a pan and bring to the boil, stirring. Then remove from the heat. Add a few drops of almond essence and stir in the soya flour, a little at a time. If the flavour is not strong enough, add more essence, kneading to mix it in evenly.

tepid milk or water if necessary. Cover the basin with a cloth, and put in a warm place until the dough has almost doubled its size (about ½ hour).

Beat thoroughly again, and then, flouring the hands, take out equal portions and shape the round buns. Place on a greased baking-sheet, allowing room for the dough to spread. Either cut a cross on top of each or use strips of shortcrust pastry to make the crosses. Put in a warm place again for about 20 minutes, until the buns are almost double in size. Bake in a hot oven (450° F.) for 15 to 20 minutes.

Lenten Savoury

6 oz. spaghetti	2 eggs, fresh or dried
¼ pint piquant white sauce	Seasoning
	¼ pint tomato sauce

(Continued on page 108)

Make your own

Pickles

By Jane Creswell
*(Combined Domestic Subjects
Diploma, Gloucester)*

While vegetables and fruit are more plentiful, do turn them into something savoury to add variety to dull meals. Full directions and recipes are given here and overleaf.

TO anyone with a garden the making of pickles is almost as serious a business as jam-making or bottling fruit—and even if you have to buy the vegetables, it's worth taking the trouble to make a few jars of pickles and chutney. Then you're sure of having something delicious and piquant in the cupboard that will make all the difference to a plate of corned beef, or bread and cheese, or the remains of a joint.

Vinegar

Vinegar is an essential ingredient in all pickles, so before you start see that you have as much in stock as you are likely to need—don't wait until you require it urgently, for there may be a temporary shortage of it then. For general purposes, brewed malt vinegar is satisfactory. Choose a good quality brand, then you can rest assured that the acetic acid content will be high enough (it should not be below 6%) to ensure that the pickles will keep. Non-brewed vinegar, even though the acetic acid content may be adequate, is only a second choice, since it has a rather crude flavour.

When you're pickling a light-coloured vegetable, such as cauliflower or onions, you may prefer a white vinegar (or a pale variety, such as wine or cider vinegar), for the sake of the colour, but when these are not obtainable ordinary malt vinegar will do quite well, and indeed it usually has a more interesting flavour than the lighter varieties.

For many recipes ' spiced vinegar ' is recommended —this is vinegar in which spices have been infused. Take whatever kind of vinegar you are going to use, and to each quart of it add ¼ oz. each of some or all of the following : cloves, peppercorns, allspice, chillies, blade mace, mustard seed and root ginger (or, if you don't keep a stock of these spices, you can buy them already mixed, as pickling spice). Bring just to the boil in a covered pan, then remove from the heat and allow to stand until the vinegar is flavoured before removing the spices—about two hours is usually sufficient. Then the vinegar is ready for use. If preferred, the spices may be included in the pickle, either loose or tied in a small muslin bag and placed in the top of each jar.

Brining

This is an important step and must not be omitted. Its purpose is to draw out some of the water from the tissues of the vegetables—if this were not done, the vinegar would be diluted too much and the pickles would not keep. There are two methods of brining— dry brining, that is, sprinkling with salt, which is suitable for watery vegetables such as marrow or cucumber, and wet brining, that is, soaking in brine, for drier vegetables such as cauliflower or onions. The brine is made in the proportion of 1 lb. salt to 1 gallon cold water. Whichever method is used, it is advisable to rinse the vegetables thoroughly afterwards, or the pickle may taste very salty. Incidentally, though most vegetables are pickled raw, root vegetables, such as artichokes, are cooked until just tender in the brine (half-strength in this case), before pickling.

Covering

The vegetables, brined, rinsed and drained, are packed into the jars and covered with the vinegar. It is always advisable to add more than is necessary to cover them, to allow for the evaporation which is likely to take place unless the jars are very tightly covered. For sealing, you can use corks (sterilised by boiling in water for a few minutes), lined with waxed paper, or tied down with parchment paper. Store in a cool dry place to mature for a while before eating. If you use metal caps for covering, you must take precautions to see that the vinegar doesn't come into contact with the metal, otherwise corrosion will take place. Line them with wax or waxed paper, or with specially prepared kerosene paper.

Mixed Pickle

For a good mixed pickle use : cauliflower, cucumber, green tomatoes, onions and marrow.

Prepare the vegetables, with the exception of the marrow, and soak in brine for twenty-four hours. Peel the marrow, remove the seeds and cut into small squares, sprinkle with salt and let stand for twelve hours. Drain the vegetables, pack, cover with cold spiced vinegar, tie down and store.

Mature at least one month before eating.

H—3

Pickled Cabbage

Use red cabbage. Remove the outer leaves, and shred finely. Place in a deep bowl, sprinkling the layers with dry salt, and leave for twenty-four hours. Drain, cover with hot spiced vinegar and leave for a further twenty-four hours, stirring occasionally. Pack and cover as usual.

Pickled Artichokes (Jerusalem)

Wash and scrape the artichokes, and cook in half-strength brine until tender but not too soft. Drain until cold. Pack in jars, cover with hot spiced vinegar, tie down and store.

Pickled Onions

Use small pickling onions. Remove the skins carefully, without cutting the onions. Wash, cover with brine and leave for twenty-four hours. Drain, wash and dry, put into jars and cover with cold spiced vinegar.

Pickled Mushrooms

1 lb. very young mushrooms
2 blades of mace
½ teaspoonful white pepper
1 teaspoonful salt
1 teaspoonful ground ginger
¼ of an onion (chopped)
Vinegar

After removing the stalks, wash the mushrooms carefully in salt water and drain well. Peel them, put into a casserole with sufficient vinegar to cover and add the rest of the ingredients. Cook in a slow oven until the mushrooms are quite tender and shrunk, lift them out, put into a bottle, and over them pour the hot vinegar. Cover and tie down.

Pickled Cauliflower

(See colour photograph on page 36)

Choose young cauliflowers, with close-flowered heads, and divide into florets, breaking rather than cutting. Cover with brine and leave to steep overnight. Next day rinse well and drain thoroughly. Then pack into jars, cover with cold spiced vinegar, and tie down.

Pickled Walnuts

Wipe the walnuts, prick well and put into a basin. Reject any that feel hard when pricked. Cover with brine and allow to soak for eight days, then throw away the brine, cover with fresh brine and resoak for fourteen days. Wash and dry well and spread the walnuts out, exposing them to the air until they turn black. Put into pickle jars and cover immediately with hot spiced vinegar. Tie down when cold. Mature from five to six weeks before using.

Popular Sweet Pickle

¾ lb. cucumber	1 oz. salt
1 lb. tomatoes	½ oz. turmeric
1½ lb. prepared marrow	¼ teaspoonful ground mace
1½ pints brown malt vinegar	¼ teaspoonful mixed spice
½ pint white malt vinegar	½ oz. bruised root ginger
¾ lb. Demerara (or white) sugar	¼ teaspoonful celery seed

Wash the cucumber, but do not peel it. Wash the tomatoes, cut in half and remove the seeds. Pass cucumber, tomatoes and marrow through a coarse mincer. Add the vinegars, sugar, salt, spices and the ginger and celery seed tied in muslin. Stir, and boil for three hours until dark in colour and of a fairly thick consistency. Cover carefully, as previously described, and store in a cool place.

Mixed Sweet Pickle

3 lb. cucumber, marrow and apples mixed	3 tablespoonfuls cloves
3 tablespoonfuls allspice	1 stick cinnamon
	2 lb. Demerara sugar

3 pints vinegar

Cut the fruit and vegetables into neat pieces, and cook in a little water until nearly tender. Drain thoroughly. Tie the spices in muslin, and boil with the sugar and vinegar for ten minutes. Add the fruit and vegetables, bring to the boil and simmer for five minutes. Drain the fruit well, and pack into hot jars. Boil the vinegar for a further ten minutes, remove the spices and pour into the jars. Cover and store.

Piccalilli

3 lb. green tomatoes
¼ cabbage
1 cauliflower
2 cucumbers
1 lb. onions
Salt
1 quart vinegar
½ lb. sugar
½ oz. turmeric
1 oz. mustard
1 teaspoonful mustard seed
1 teaspoonful peppercorns

Cut the vegetables into small pieces and place in a basin in layers, alternating with layers of salt. Allow to stand overnight and then drain. Boil together the vinegar, sugar, turmeric and mustard, with the mustard seed and peppercorns tied in a muslin bag. Add the vegetables and heat through without boiling. Remove muslin bag and pack into sterilised jars. Seal and store about a month before using.

Marrow Chutney

3 lb. marrow	12 peppercorns
Salt	¼ oz. bruised ginger, if obtainable
½ lb. shallots	4 oz. sugar
½ lb. green apples	1½ pints vinegar.
½ lb. sultanas, if obtainable	

Cut up the marrow and place in a basin. Sprinkle with two teaspoonfuls of salt; leave for twelve hours; drain and rinse. Peel and chop the shallots and apples finely. Tie the spices in muslin. Put all the ingredients in a saucepan, bring slowly to the boil and simmer gently until cooked and of the correct consistency. Remove muslin bag, pot and cover.

For further pickles and chutney recipes and for the method of salting beans, see Good Housekeeping's 'Home Bottling and Jam-Making,' price 9d. (10½d. by post) from booksellers or from the Good Housekeeping Centre, 30, Grosvenor Gardens, London, S.W.1.

WHY I HATE A

BY GAIL RICHMOND

WOULD you rather work for a man or a woman? Sooner or later, if you work at all, this question will fall upon your ears. And if you don't answer in a split second, a dozen other voices will.

"I'd never work for a woman."

"I'd never work for a man."

"Well, in some ways, perhaps I would prefer a woman."

"At all events, you know where you are with a man."

At this point someone will announce gloomily: "Not with all of them!"

Your eyes will glance from speaker to speaker in the manner of eyes watching tennis on the centre-court. It's amazing the amount of conversational volleying this question invariably provokes. Usually, unless you have definite ideas of your own, you're left with the impression you'll back the wrong horse if you ever decide to work for a woman.

Women are temperamental. If they're happy, their lives running smoothly, they make satisfactory bosses most of the time.

But if a love affair has turned a wrong corner, if they loathe a new hat or the jam made on Sunday hasn't set, you're for it.

A woman can't handle staff without getting a power complex. She loves being an autocrat. The office is the only place she ever has a chance. She won't let you in on the broader aspects of the job in case you learn too much and finish by beating her at her own job.

She's a cat. "Why don't you use a little rouge, Miss Jones? It's such an improvement."

"I know you've told me your mother's delicate, but couldn't you possibly get here on time more often?"

"After all, I have all the responsibility, surely you could remember to change the calendar."

A woman who works for a woman may find all these charges true, and a lot more. She will find herself constantly impaled upon another woman's moods and have to combat her own at the same time.

A woman boss can be a fault-finding executive all morning, return from a suc-

{Wo}man Boss

ILLUSTRATED BY PEARL FALCONER

I'd never work for a man ...

He is too impersonal

He's moody

He's inconsiderate ...

He has exasperating habit

cessful lunch and let down her back hair and be 'just another girl.' In this state of mind she is quite likely to ask wildly embarrassing questions about your private life, draw out confessions that you never wanted to make, and give you a great deal of totally useless advice, inspired in these cosy moments by her present view of her own experience.

The next day you have an uncomfortable idea she has forgotten nothing you told her and is storing it up to use against you on some future occasion. Very often she is.

She may also be tight about money. A great many women executives are. They keep as eagle an eye on pay cheques and other office expenses as they would if compelled by a spendthrift or impecunious husband to be careful over the housekeeping.

This type of woman hates asking for a rise on your account, or giving you one on her own, and unless you fly in the face of authority and speak for yourself, or get a better job, there's precious little you can do about it. She can also be a fiend on the question of holidays. You're entitled to two weeks, but when you raise the question of which two weeks, she gives you a glance as if she'd caught you stealing.

"It's too early to decide. I'm too busy at the moment. You'll have to wait. I don't know when I'm going yet."

If you try to pin her down she is liable to announce superciliously: "You seem to forget I have this office to run."

A woman is never impersonal about her job. Well, she rarely is. One particularly common expression is to make the office another dear little home. She puts flowers on her desk, hangs paintings on the wall, and when she receives callers plays the rôle of hostess and makes it clear that her secretary is parlourmaid.

"Make some tea, Miss Jones, and there are some of my own home-made biscuits in the cupboard."

Twitter, twitter! Look at me in my office, but I'm proving I'm a woman at heart.

Men, on the other hand, are admitted as being much more stable. Yet where is

(Continued on page 90)

H—2

*Pad those
shoulders well*

*Wear gored skirts,
placket in front*

*Be neat and trim —
with a squared cut
smock and slim skirt*

*A small, soft
pillow helps*

those changing

ARE you expecting a small addition to your family? Here
are some suggestions to help you to look well and feel
well during the months of waiting, without incurring a lot
of expense.

Buy two smocks, each a size larger than usual, and pleated
—they hang more becomingly. Then pad the shoulders and
bust well. Don't be squeamish about discreetly upholstering
your top. Choose a plain, but not dismal, colour and if you
prefer flowered patterns, have one with a dark background.

Take one of your old gored skirts and wear it with the
placket in front. At the waist sew a loop of tape to hook
into the fastening at the waistband, leaving the ends to let
out as your measurements increase. In this way you will find
the skirt gives the appearance of hanging from a slim
waist.

Take particular care with your make-up and grooming.
Wear a decorative hat, gay scarf or small colourful

Carry on ~ as usual

Step out ~ stride,
don't paddle ~ in
low-heeled shoes

Curves

brooch, and carry a large handbag at waist level. Wear your clothes with assurance and poise. As with your smocks, keep the shoulders of your swagger coat well padded and wear low-heeled shoes. In other words, fuss about your top and people will forget your girth.

Unless advised by your doctor, don't wear a maternity corset. If you need support, get two 3-in. crêpe bandages and bind yourself with them, not tightly but evenly and comfortably. In the last stages, bind them sling fashion to help to keep the weight off your pelvis. Get a 2-in. wide elastic belt to wear over the hips and fasten your suspenders to this.

In bed at night a small soft cushion under your side often helps you to relax. Wear a brassière at night as well as during the day. Rest, but not too much; live a normal life, take enough exercise—brisk walks are excellent—and the time will fly past.

Rest ~ but
not too much

"What Shall We Give Them to Eat?"
(*Continued from page* **41**)—taste and red or orange colouring. Pour jelly into 10 conical-shaped wine-glasses. Allow to set.

Clown Faces: Mix cornflour and sugar to a paste with a little cold milk. Boil the remainder of the milk and add the blended cornflour. Cook for a few minutes, add the vanilla, and pour into 10 wine-glasses, egg-cups or other containers of suitable size. Put in a cool place to set. (If cornflour is unobtainable use 2½ oz. flour instead or from ¾–2 oz. gelatine according to type used.)

Frills: On 10 pieces of paper mark two rounds, the outer the size of a saucer and the inner about 2–3 inches in diameter. Cut out and pleat, painting every other ridge with some culinary colouring—or, if the food does not touch that part, with black ink.

Putting them together: Turn cornflour moulds on to jelly bases. Arrange frills around. Make eyes and nose with small pieces of liquorice and mouth with a piece of carrot.

Place ice-cream cones (they can be made of paper) on top at a jaunty angle.

If ice-cream in cones can be purchased immediately before the party this can replace the cornflour moulds.

'Alphabet Bricks' and Iced Cake

1 lb. self-raising flour
2 tablespoonfuls dried egg
3 oz. sugar
½ teaspoonful salt
1 teaspoonful baking powder
4 oz. lard
¼ pint syrup
1 level tablespoonful cocoa
½ teaspoonful cochineal
4 oz. dried fruit
¼–½ pint water or milk to mix

Sieve flour, egg, sugar, salt and baking powder. Warm fat and syrup until melted, and add to sieved ingredients. Stir in sufficient milk or water to make a pouring consistency. Sieve in cocoa and pour cochineal in the centre. Stir in a circular motion to mix partially—leaving the mixture in a streaky condition. Pour half into a square or oblong tin for the bricks. Add dried fruit to the remainder and stir so that the colour is uniform. Pour into a round tin for the iced cake. Bake both in a slow to moderate oven (300–350° F.) for 1–1½ hours.

Bricks: Cut into neat squares, cover with differently coloured icings and pipe with letters—preferably the children's initials.

Iced Cake: Coat with chocolate icing. Surround with a gay cake frill.

Banana Sandwiches

2–3 bananas
2 oz. butter
2–3 tablespoonfuls blackcurrant purée
1 small loaf

Mash the bananas, mix with blackcurrant purée and melted butter. Cut a small loaf in thin slices lengthwise. Cut off crusts. Spread with the mixture and roll up like a swiss roll.

THE INSTITUTE'S
Party Table

Snow scene to delight the children specially designed by Peter Luling
(*who directs the Furnishing Studio*)

As a base for the snow scene (photographed in colour opposite) the lid of a wooden box, about 20 inches by 16 inches, was used, with strips of wood tacked to the sides to make an edge. Any large tray would do equally well. To represent the frozen pond, a sheet of blue paper covered with Cellophane was laid down and the landscape was built up round it with earth from the garden. Most of this was covered with moss to represent bushes and evergreen trees. The house was very simply made from card, with a roof of corrugated cardboard. Carefully chosen twigs realistically represent bare winter trees with a few touches of white paint for snow on the branches. Lastly, a little talcum powder (any white powder could be used) was sprinkled here and there to represent snow, and small figures modelled in Plasticine were added. The blue tablecloth came from Heal and Son, Ltd.

* * *

Jellied Rabbit

1½–3 oz. gelatine (according to type used)
¼ pint cold water
¼ pint rose-hip syrup
1 tablespoonful golden syrup
1 teaspoonful lemonade crystals
Few drops raspberry flavouring
1 teaspoonful red colouring
Water up to 1½ pints

Soak gelatine in cold water. Melt over hot. Add rose-hip syrup, syrup and lemonade crystals. Stir until dissolved. Make up to 1½ pints. Add flavouring to taste, and colouring. Pour into a bunny mould. Put in a cool place to set, and serve on chopped-up green jelly to look like grass.

Chocolate and Apple Snow

2 oz. cornflour (or custard powder or oatflour)
1 tablespoonful sugar
1 tablespoonful cocoa
¾ pint milk
¼ pint evaporated milk
1–2 teaspoonfuls vanilla

Apple Snow

½–1 oz. gelatine (according to type used)
3 tablespoonfuls cold water
½ lb. apples
1 tablespoonful sugar
Water to cover
Lemon squash or water—up to ½ pint
Green Jelly

Chocolate Mould: Blend cornflour, sugar and cocoa with a little cold milk. Boil the remaining milk and add to blended cornflour. Return to saucepan and cook for a few minutes; add evaporated milk and vanilla. Pour into a wetted sandwich cake-tin; put in a cool place to set. When cold (and do not leave too long, for the tin tends to mark the chocolate) turn out.

Apple Snow: Soak gelatine in cold water. Melt over hot. Core and peel apples. Cook fruit with sugar in sufficient water to cover. Add soaked gelatine. Stir until dissolved. (*Continued on page* **88**)

Colour photograph by Chaloner Woods, F.I.B.P.

A—5

Young and gay

Cardigan suit in Bedford cord, £18 4s. 2d., 18 coupons. Matching slacks, £5 19s. 4d., 8 coupons; in Scarlet, Turquoise, Grey, Black, Navy, Light Blue, Straw and Yellow. Wool Blouse £4 4s., 6 coupons, in several lovely colours. All from Jaeger Shops

should men do HOUSEWORK?

Do things go to pot when you're away or have to take to your bed?

If you split the burden of household chores now, your husband will

know how to keep body, soul and shirts together in an emergency

A STORY is current that a certain British sergeant, returning from the wars, found his wife in the act of cleaning the windows.

"That's not the way to do it," he exclaimed in horror, taking the chamois-cloth out of her hand. "You use too much water!"

And forthwith he began to polish the window to high and beautiful transparency.

The poor wife fainted from shock! Resuscitated at length, she explained that never previously had she known her husband do a stroke of housework. Before the war he had, in fact, been so lazy that he had wanted her to blacken all the windows.

Possibly this story contains an element of exaggeration, but it does emphasise the fact that thousands of ex-Service men have returned home with unprecedented experience of the traditional feminine duties of washing, ironing, cleaning and cooking—qualified, as never before, to be true partners in the task of making a home. But are they gladly taking upon their newly trained shoulders an equitable share of housework? And if not, why not?

The fault, one man declares, lies with the women. "They always adopt the wrong tactics!"

If you want him to be a real 'partner in home-making' he advises:

1. Look for the job he can do better than you can. Frankly admit his greater success and don't be ashamed to learn from him.

2. Don't stand over him, always giving directions.

3. Don't ridicule and remember his mistakes.

4. If his sense of 'fairness' makes him share household tasks, go out of your way to help him with matters in which he is interested.

the Navy says 'YES!'

If you think the tale that men can do house-

work happily, is too good to be true, read the

post-war experiences of this mother of two sailors

ONCE upon a time I was proud mother of two small boys. But *what* boys! Untidy, dirty, always coming in from garden or fields and flinging down muddy shoes and torn coats anywhere and anyhow. My round of mending, washing and cleaning was unending.

Then came the war, and my two sons entered the Navy—the Service of all Services for teaching the things I had been unable to teach them, little ways that will make them welcome guests in any home without domestic staff.

Now mornings start well. The sons get up at first call or, better still, wake themselves and even get breakfast for me.

They make their beds, leave their rooms tidy, clothes in little piles (the Navy seems to love things in little rolled-up piles) and shoes left side by side like loving couples.

Washing-up is done in record time—knives, forks and spoons lined up in tidy rows and the wearisome task enlivened by good rollicking songs in which we all join.

They insist on washing their own clothes, or perhaps I should say doing their 'dhobi.' Ironing at any rate, I thought, (Continued on page 40)

H—3

YOU Needn't HAVE "PUPPYFAT"

BEFORE. This was Julie, in her teens, five feet five tall, pretty face, shiny hair: so far so good. But she weighed 10 st. 6 lb., unquestionably too much. So she went in for some sane slimming. . . .

IT'S a fallacy that teen-age plumpness is unavoidable. Your figure is made by the food you eat, and—unless you suffer from gland trouble—what you don't put *in*, you can't put *on*. Most fattening of all are sweetstuffs and starchy foods: bread, potatoes, pastries, cakes, suet or milky puddings. So, if you mean business, cut these first. No need to bore your family and friends with your diet plans: simply eat one slice of toast instead of three at breakfast, one potato instead of two at lunch, and be strong-minded about refusing sweets and snacks. Don't cut out fats: you need these for your health's sake.

Two months' care can trim your figure incredibly. And while you work towards weighing what a pretty teen-ager should, study these points.

These make you look fatter

Poor posture. A slump that thickens you through the middle. Feet wide apart, a fat-lady stance that spreads your hips.

Sloppy grooming. Any lack of cleanness, neatness, freshness.

A bushy hair-do. This can make your head look immense.

Lines going round you, such as wide or contrasting belts.

Some dress materials. Transparent or clinging stuffs. Too-thick tweeds. Large prints.

These make you look slimmer

Standing tall to pull yourself up to your longest lines. Chest up, to slim that middle region. Straight back. Seat tucked under. Feet together, toes pointed ahead, for graceful legs.

Faultless grooming. Meticulous cleanness to make you look good enough to eat. Determined steps, if necessary, to overcome the perspiration problem. Finicky attention to hair and finger-nails.

A clear, healthy skin, and bright eyes, and a cheerful smile, so that people forget your curves.

A smooth hair-do, well brushed.

Soft, dull-textured materials in plain darkish colours.

Simple shoes. The plain, slim court shoe is best of all.

Muriel Cox, Beauty Editor

AFTER. This is Julie two months later. Two months of "No" to snacks and sweets, extra helpings and fat-making foods. The time seemed very long, but she's delighted now.

Waistline. Lying on floor, back flat, touch opposite hands and toes

Hips. Hands on hips, 'bicycle' with legs in air. Repeat lying on side

Thighs. Holding chair-back for balance, swing the legs in wide circles

Ankle. Roll each ankle 20 times, toes describing as big a circle as possible

the Basement room

A basement kitchen becomes a family games room, cheerfully decorated at little cost

BASEMENT rooms are a problem which many town-dwellers must face, whether they like it or not. Relics of a society and a design for living as dead as good Queen Anne, there they still remain like half-buried white elephants.

In a very small family-house it may be necessary to keep the basement kitchen as such, and in this case the best plan is to use the adjoining room for dining.

In the middle size family-house, or the large house converted into flats, the kitchen or kitchens will be upstairs. After adequate storage space has been provided, one or two rooms will still be left empty. Basement flats, whether for tenants or caretakers, are unacceptable by modern standards, and it is to be hoped that they will eventually disappear. How then can the basement room be fitted into the economy of the house and made of practical use?

Our solution is that it should become a family games room, a room without furniture that can be 'spoilt,' with provision for hobbies and entertainments. In a house converted into flats, such a room might belong to one of them or might even be 'communal.' The main essential is that it shall be warm and well-lit, to make up for the lack of natural daylight.

In the scheme illustrated above, a basement kitchen, about 15 ft. square, has been inexpensively converted. The walls are distempered ivory white and the ceiling golden yellow, to give a feeling of light and warmth. The removal of the old kitchen range leaves a large, open hearth, which is fitted with a 'fire-basket' for burning coal or logs, and on either side low seats have been built out in brick. Brick has also been used to make the front of the seats in the recesses at either side, which have hinged tops so that they can be used as lockers. The upholstery is covered in cotton duck dyed Indian-red. The recesses are lit from above by screened fluorescent tubes, and the walls covered by photostatic enlargements of large-scale ordnance maps of the district, which have been painted. Such enlargements can be made at a cost of no more than a pound or two, and any print or picture

KENRICK

can be enlarged in the same way. Above the fireplace is a screen for cinema or magic-lantern shows.

On the right, the old kitchen dresser has been kept, and can serve as a work bench. The table and forms have been made from the tops of old Army tables, which can be bought for 10s. to 14s. each. Four will be needed to make a table of this pattern and two forms. Wood from the same source has been used for the indoor shutters of the window, which have been painted in stripes. Fibre matting on the floor, and a tub chair made from a barrel, complete the sturdy furnishing of this room.

GOOD HOUSEKEEPING FURNISHING STUDIO

30 Grosvenor Gardens, London, S.W.1

* **Directed by Peter Luling** *

The **Exhibition of 'Further Furnishings for To-day'** will remain open until the end of April, Monday to Friday, 9.30 a.m. to 5 p.m. The **Exhibition** of individually framed prints and modern colour reproductions has been unavoidably postponed until May

Use your Easter eggs to make this custard pie. (Recipe overleaf)

GOOD HOUSEKEEPING
INSTITUTE

FURNITURE

Top left : Chippendale mahogany chair (about 1755). Above : Curves, carving and knick-knacks of the Victorian period. Left and below right : Desk, chair and easy chair designed by Christopher Heal. Below left : Contemporary table and Windsor chairs

LOUISE MORGAN goes behind the scenes, visiting factories, large and small, to report on this little-publicised but most important subject

*As bright and homely
as a patchwork quilt,
this scheme will suit
any small attic room*

**Designed by
Charles Kenrick**

IF anyone feels that life in an attic lacks dignity he can console himself by remembering the origin of the word. Meaning literally 'of Athens,' it stands for all that is most classically beautiful. How it came to have its present domestic sense is a curious story. When classical architecture was revived in England, any building in this style was naturally described as 'Attic.' Gradually the word was narrowed down to refer to one typical feature, where one small 'order' or column is placed above a taller one, and hence to the highest storey of a house. Soon everybody boasted the elegance of an attic, no matter what the shape of their house, and the earlier term 'garret' was too vulgar for a room in any respectable home. At the same time another upper room seems to have disappeared. Dr. Johnson, in his Dictionary, has it that the garret is the room above the cock-loft. But if you search the same source to find out what a cock-loft may have been, you will find it described as the room above the garret!

However, it matters little which came over which, since we are too refined now to have garrets, and cock-lofts have gone also—perhaps because neighbours complained of the cock-crows.

There is a peculiar charm to attic rooms shared by no other floor of the house. Partly it is due to the bird's-eye view from the windows, with its foreground of tree-tops and chimney-pots; partly to the peaceful seclusion that rewards one for a climb to the very top. Above all, it is the homely shape of the rooms, small, low-ceilinged and with sloping walls, that gives even a London attic the intimacy of a country cottage.

However, these informal charms are often accompanied by a considerable amount of discomfort and practical inconvenience. Originally intended for the humblest members of the household, little thought and less expenditure was in the past devoted to these rooms. In some Victorian houses this may have advantages, as there will be an absence of bad ornament, elaborate fireplaces, mouldings and picture rails. But there

the Attic room

is usually also an absence of cupboards and hanging space, and sloping walls and the haphazard relation of doors and windows make the arrangement of furniture difficult. Yet the sloping walls and odd-shaped corners make the fitting of built-in cupboards, shelves and other fitments particularly easy.

In our furnishing scheme for this month we have illustrated a typical attic room with sloping walls and dormer window on one side. Against these walls simple cupboards have been built which can be used partly for hanging and partly for shelves, and leave space for a row of books above. By coming out farther from the wall, a full-length cupboard can be provided in one corner.

Between these fitments and below the window a dressing-table shelf has been constructed, extending slightly to each side of the dormer, with curtains below. Muslin curtains only have been used for the window, with a gathered pelmet to match, so as to cut off as little light as possible. The colour scheme is as bright and unsophisticated as a cottage garden. Brilliant red floor felt, pale yellow-green wallpaper, green-and white candy-stripe chintz. The paintwork is white.

The 'cottagey' character of the room is main-

GOOD HOUSEKEEPING

FURNISHING STUDIO

30 *Grosvenor Gardens, London, S.W.*1

directed by Peter Luling

tained in the furniture. There is nothing modern here, and nothing elaborate or costly. The serpentine-fronted chest of drawers is the show piece, but could be replaced by something simpler—perhaps a plain chest painted white. The rest of the furniture is unassuming; a chair of Hepplewhite character, a small pedestal table, a Victorian armchair with a new cover of the striped chintz, a piano stool used before the dressing-table. An informal collection such as this, without any coherence of period, seems right for this cheerful and homely room.

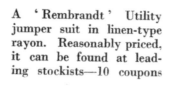

A 'Rembrandt' Utility jumper suit in linen-type rayon. Reasonably priced, it can be found at leading stockists—10 coupons

Black barathea suit from L. G. Cooper's 'Couture Clothes' range. It costs £20 and 18 coupons; from several good stores

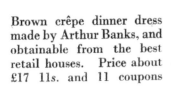

Brown crêpe dinner dress made by Arthur Banks, and obtainable from the best retail houses. Price about £17 11s. and 11 coupons

A cosy all-purpose coat by 'Windsmoor' in angora and wool, costing about £17 and 18 coupons. D. H. Evans have it in stock

THE INSTITUTE
Experiments

Above : Using the apparatus of the scientist—balances, beakers, measuring cylinder, bunsen burner, thermometer—Good Housekeeping Institute tests the properties of a new food product. Below : Then the scientific data are converted into simple directions which any busy housewife can immediately understand

EXPERIMENT and research are the background of all Institute activities, and day in, day out, the 'back-room' staff are investigating new domestic problems. Always the method of attack is similar.

First, experimental work. Only when the necessary basic information has been acquired does the cookery expert take over, to convert, as it were, the scientific experiment into the useful recipe or time-saving hint which eventually finds its place in the Institute pages of GOOD HOUSEKEEPING Magazine.

We think you may like to know something about this work and the infinite care taken in compiling recipes and instructions, and so we propose telling you about some of the subjects which have engaged the attention of our research staff recently.

When a new food or an old one in a new form, such as Potato Mash Powder, comes into being, experiments, sometimes detailed and complex, sometimes very simple, as in this case, must be carried out to find out just how the new product should be used. Whether simple or complex, such experimental work can make all the difference to the housewife.

Preliminary testing with accurate balances, measuring cylinders, thermometers, is often needed, as, for instance, with Potato Mash Powder, before really practical instructions for use can be drawn up. The busy housewife obviously has no time to conduct her own experiments, nor can she risk culinary failures. She wants homely measures and simple directions which will enable her to produce quickly attractive and interesting dishes.

The instructions provided with the Potato Mash Powder stated : " Add $\frac{1}{4}$ pint of nearly boiling water to $1\frac{1}{4}$ oz. Potato Mash Powder while stirring rapidly." A $\frac{1}{4}$ oz. weight has a way of losing itself or, still worse, scales sensitive enough to weigh such a small amount accurately may not be available. We felt, therefore, that homely measures such as tablespoonfuls should be substituted for weight.

Then came the question of the temperature of the water. How important was it to add the water to the powder, or might it be better to reverse this procedure? (Continued on page 40)

No.1 Potato Mash Powder

2d ON THE RATES!

E. Dixon Grubb tells us what we get for our money

WHEN the grocer sends his account, we check each item on the bill. If he has charged for two pounds of sugar, we make sure that two pounds of sugar have been delivered. If he has charged us for best quality goods, we make sure that nothing cheaper has been substituted. That is what every tradesman expects us to do. The man who serves us well wants us to know it; and it is in his interest, as well as our own, to check the bill.

This applies to the rate demand as well as to tradesmen's accounts. We have a right to know how our money is spent. That is why the law insists that every Local Authority shall print details on the back of the demand note. It is one of the duties of ordinary townspeople to decide whether the councillors are spending too much, or too little, on running our services for us.

Women are not brainy enough to understand the financial side of Local Government? Rubbish! Housewives who cope successfully every day of their lives with points values, bread units, ration cards and clothing coupons, in addition to balancing the household budget, need not fear the complications of municipal finance.

In fact, ordinary women—not just the few who become councillors—are the deciding factor. There is hardly a town in the country where women do not outnumber men on the municipal voting lists. So when (Continued on page 116)

Dr. to

LOCAL GOVERNMENT UNLTD.

PARTNERS { BLANKSHIRE COUNTY COUNCIL
{ LITTLEBOROUGH CORPORATION

Mr. A.N.Y. Citizen

Services rendered during week ending 27 July 1947

£. s. d

	£	s	d
Use of schools and libraries	9	6½	
Use of clean roads and streets	4		
Public Health Services	4	2	
Relief of needy families	2	2¾	
Sending men to empty dustbin		3¾	
Unlimited supply of water at tap		4¾	
Protection from burglars & other police service	4	1¾	
Housing & Town Planning		2¾	
Maternity & child welfare		2	
Use of Parks and Public Buildings			
Miscellaneous Services			
Cost of collection & office expenses			
TOTAL:	**3**	**0**	

LITTLEBOROUGH CORPORATION,

DEMAND NOTE FOR GENERAL RATE & WATER RATE

Mr. A. N. Y. Citizen,
15 Typical Road,
LITTLEBOROUGH.

(or Occupier)

1

The Littleborough Corporation demand payment of a **General Rate** at 7/6 in the £ also the half-yearly **Water Rate** in respect of the financial half-year ending 30th September, 1945, NOW DUE FROM YOU.

Number in Rate Book	Hereditaments (if other than that specified in Address)	Net Annual Value (where it differs from Rateable Value) £ s.	Rateable Value £	General Rate at 7/6 in the £ s. d.
834	Dwelling House,		28	10 10 -
	Total General Rate ... ... £			10 10 -

save up for Easter

Even at Easter-time there are seldom quite as many eggs as we might want, and the Institute has been thinking up ways of making a few look like many.

For a while before Easter, empty eggs by making a ring of holes with a needle at the pointed end. If you make these holes carefully, very close together, the piece (about the size of a sixpence) will fall out, leaving an almost whole shell which can be used in all manner of intriguing ways.

They can, for instance, be filled with fondant. This is an exciting novelty for children, and the fondant eggs could be used for the traditional Easter Egg Hunt with which many families start the day.

FONDANT EGGS

1 lb. sugar	¼ pint water	Colouring and flavouring

Choose a thick-bottomed pan, dissolve the sugar in the water, add colour and flavouring if desired, and bring to the boil. Cook for 30 to 40 minutes, stirring all the time. Test by dropping a little of the mixture into cold water. When it can be formed into soft balls, it is ready. Wash the empty shells thoroughly. Fill them with fondant, replace the tops and leave to harden.

TABLE DECORATION

Shells can be used, too, for table decoration. Again they must be thoroughly washed and wiped, if possible, with methylated spirit, to make sure there is no grease on them. Then paint on amusing faces and make hats and curls of gay paper, which a touch of gum will keep securely in place. If plain white egg-cups are used, suitable (or amusing) clothes can be painted on this "body," to promote still further the idea of stumpy little people.

Thick, ordinary water-colours, or vegetable dyes such as are used for colouring icing, can be applied with a paint-brush. Those who feel that such artistic embellishments are beyond them can safely content themselves with adding paper hats only. These delight children, whose vivid imaginations soon supply the missing features.

Brightly dyed eggs give colour
to your Easter breakfast table

Colour Photograph by Chaloner Woods, F.I.B.P.

how to cook green vegetables

For delicious flavour and fine health qualities, vegetables grown in this country cannot be beaten. The simple modern way of cooking gives you greens that are refreshingly *green*, tender yet crisp, delicate in flavour ; greens, moreover, that retain the greatest possible amount of their valuable vitamin C—the vitamin that helps so much to give clear skin and bright eyes, and that keeps you feeling fit and vigorous.

1 Wash the greens thoroughly but *quickly*. Cut cabbages into quarters to make washing easier ; the looser " spring greens " type can be opened with the fingers and worked about in the water. Don't soak green vegetables, as this draws out some of the valuable Vitamin C and mineral salts.

2 Cut out the stump of cabbage, remove coarse stalks of other greens. Then shred the greens coarsely with a sharp knife. Remember, the sooner they go from the garden or shop into the pot, the more flavour and health value greens give you. So don't buy or prepare them sooner than you need.

3 Put only enough water in the saucepan to prevent burning—about a teacupful for each 2 lb. greens. Add a little salt and bring water to the boil. When it is boiling *fast* put in the greens and shut down the lid tightly. This is most important.

4 Boil for only 10-15 minutes shaking the pan occasionally to prevent sticking. Drain, and serve the greens at once. Keeping hot or re-heating destroys vitamin C. Save any liquid for soups or sauces — it's good, and good for you!

POINTS TO REMEMBER

Over-cooking, cooking in too much water and cooking with the lid off make vegetables soggy and yellow, emits an unpleasant " cabbage-y " smell and wastes precious vitamin C. Shredding large-leaved green vegetables enables them to cook faster, so saves flavour and health values.

BRUSSELS SPROUTS. Remove any old stump or outer leaves, make a criss-cross cut in the stump end of the sprout. Wash thoroughly. Cook small sprouts whole. Large sprouts may be cut in halves. Cook as directed above, *and for not more than 15-20 minutes.*

BROCCOLI should be shredded, CAULIFLOWER broken into sprigs. SPINACH needs no water other than that which clings to it after washing; otherwise cook as other greens, being especially careful to shake the pan occasionally to prevent sticking. (C 12)

ISSUED BY THE MINISTRY OF FOOD

THE Silver Year

BY CLIFFORD BAX

Bippu

On a day of April in 1948 our King and Queen will have been married for twenty-five years. To anyone who is still on the green side of forty, such a span of time may seem immense. To anyone who, like me, has surprised him or herself by becoming sixty, that wedding-day— April 26th, 1923—does not seem very far away. I still catch myself thinking, " And the Duke of York, who recently played lawn-tennis at Wimbledon, fell in love with that pretty Scots lady in her family's famous old castle, and how obviously it was a love-match. . . . I can't remember whether the Duke was quite so successful on the tennis-court ? "

And then, when their first baby was born, we —poets, housemaids and all other romantic persons—were as much delighted as though we were forty million uncles, aunts or cousins of the miniature princess. Of course, we could not then guess that before many years had flowed past she would suddenly find herself heir-presumptive to Britain's ancient throne. How I pity those lean and hungry Cassiuses unable to comprehend our sentiment about the Royal Family. They miss much—a great deal more than they realise. I believe that when modern psychology has advanced a little further we shall all recognise that the notion and the reality of kingship and queenship are almost necessary to the health of the " unconscious " mind.

A crown, for example, must be a symbol extremely familiar to those intrepid professors who explore the dreams and fantasies of their clients. There is in each of us a dream-king or a dream-queen who represents the Ideal Person

whom we should like to be, and that is, if I am right, the deep origin of our veneration for a queen or a king. Sometimes in the past a royal person has let us down, and such a person not only damages our ideal but finds that we do not easily forgive him. On the other hand, how inspiring it is when a royal person is naturally regal. . . . I do not think, for example, that anyone can have conversed with Queen Mary and have come away with the feeling that royalty is " just mumbo-jumbo." Indeed, if the Edwardian millionaires and aristocrats had shared Queen Mary's lively interests in the arts they could easily have placed Great Britain at the top of the cultural scale in the world. Unfortunately most of them were self-satisfied philistines.

King George and Queen Elizabeth have not had easy lives. He has not spent his time in " counting out his money," and she has had little leisure for " eating bread and honey." As Duke and (Continued on page 86)

BY BRIGID MAXWELL

It's Happening This Summer

A Guide to Britain's Summer Season for 1948— which promises, despite restrictions, to be the gayest and most eventful for many years

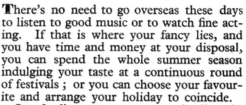

Festivals

There's no need to go overseas these days to listen to good music or to watch fine acting. If that is where your fancy lies, and you have time and money at your disposal, you can spend the whole summer season indulging your taste at a continuous round of festivals ; or you can choose your favourite and arrange your holiday to coincide.

Stratford's season opens on April 15th, with " King John," and from then, right on till the beginning of October, the Bard is on the boards.

The " Birthday " play this year will be " Hamlet," on April 23rd. " The Merchant of Venice," " The Taming of the Shrew," " The Winter's Tale," " Troilus and Cressida," and " Othello " are all billed. Diana Wynyard will be leading lady—her first appearance at the Festival.

Those who visit Stratford—and 238,000 people did, last year—can wander by the green-edged Avon, read again in ancient stone and timber the history of Shakespeare's England, dine in the much-discussed Memorial Theatre's spacious restaurant before the show, and combine, as it were, the best of art and nature. An early August visitor will probably become involved in the English Folk Song and Dance Society's summer Festival. Some of the dances take place in the streets, and innocent passers-by are apt to be " swep' away " too.

Up North, from August 22nd to September 11th, will be held the festival of festivals —Edinburgh's second International Festival of Music and Drama. Last year it broke all records for home and overseas visitors. It has a unique (Continued on page 90)

Sport

Fairs

Do you like watching other people being energetic? If the answer is "Yes," this next six months might have been planned for you. Not for years has there been such a programme of sport in Britain. The Australians are coming—to retain, they hope, the Ashes they won in 1946. The Olympic Games will draw crowds from all over the world. And, in addition, there will be the annual glories of Epsom, Wimbledon, Ascot, Bisley, Henley and Cowes.

The Australian tour will start, as always, with a match on Worcester's small but charming ground at the end of April. England, say the pundits, has little hope of wresting the Ashes from the Aussies this year—but there is always the chance. And there is always the incomparable Mr. Compton, who has used his bat before now to work miracles.

The five Tests will take place, as usual, at Nottingham, Lords, Manchester, Leeds and the Oval during June, July and August. The visitors will play county matches, too, so there will be ample opportunity to watch their skill. There are heretics who consider cricket a dull game. Let them look up records which show that during the classic match at the Oval in '83, when Australia won by 7 runs, the excitement was so intense that one spectator dropped dead and another gnawed the head completely off his umbrella!

It seems a pity that the Tests are of necessity played in cities, for cricket looks best against a rural background. For those who think of combining a Test with a quiet holiday, the best bet is, *(Continued on page 94)*

The Arts and Sport having had their turns, what of the folk who fashion the background of everyday life with hand and brain—the farmers, industrialists, gardeners, soldiers, sailors. . . . They have entertainment to offer, too, this summer.

Since agriculture, with mining, ranks as the country's most important industry, let's see what the farmers are up to. You'll see it, of course, as you travel the green countryside, but if you want it in concentrated form, then visit York early in July—from the 6th to the 9th; or Cardiff at the end of May; or Inverness towards the end of June. In each of these places is held one of the country's big Agricultural Shows.

Greatest of all is "The Royal"—the Show of the Royal Agricultural Society of England. It will be held this year in an open space of about one hundred acres, called Knavesmire, near York Racecourse. It lasts for four days, and so great was its popularity last year—the first "Royal" since the war—that many farmers complained they could not get near the exhibits and stock-judging because the world and his wife had got there first. It may be that at York only *bona fide* farming folk will be admitted on the first day.

The show is in two main parts: livestock judging and exhibits. Horses, cattle, pigs, poultry, goats and sheep are the competitors. Horses alone divide into 15 different classes, from ponies to percherons. *(Continued on page 97)*

DECORATION BY JAMES HART

the answer's in *the positive*

Photograph by Baron—these three words began to appear under pictures in well-known English periodicals in the years before the war. When Britain began to get back into its bowler hat again after the conflict, there they were again, the observant began to notice.

Who, they began to ask, is Baron? Is that his real name or a title used as an incognito? Is he a member of some noble house with family prestige behind him?

For once curiosity was well justified. Life's most intriguing stories are not always told in the largest letters. Behind this trio, in their modest italic type, lie the hopes and fears, endeavours, disappointments, discoveries and successes of a young man who had the courage to walk out of a flourishing family business and launch out into the deep on his own account. Work in his father's firm, he says, was dull! In other words, it gave him scope only to achieve easy affluence, but not to use to the full the talents and initiative with which time has proved he was well endowed.

But to tell his story aright, I must first explain that he is *not the holder of a title.* Baron is just his Christian name, and is followed by the surname Nahum. His father was a Manchester businessman of Dutch origin, engaged in the (Continued on page 86)

by DAVID MILLS

1 Prince Philip—" I like this one best," says Baron.
2 Showing Jack la Rue how to die for the camera.
3 Almost perfect composition.
4 First of a series for De Reszke cigarette advertisements.
5 Chico Marx at the London Casino.
6 Table at Brooks's cut to fit Charles James Fox.
7 The Mountbattens sat out in the snow for this picture.
8 Baron by Baron—all done with mirrors !
9 Another mirror shot—French playwright, Yves Mirande.
10 " My favourite picture of Margot Fonteyn."
11 Roland Young in " Bond Street."
12 Sally Gray—" one of our most photogenic stars."

7. A " Blanes " suit—slender, hip-draped, coolly elegant in rayon crêpe. At Harvey Nichols, £7 8s. 4d., 10 coupons. The hat, distractingly pretty in rough straw, by Gertrude Harris

More engaging Summery Dresses on page 29

satisfy good appetites with

fish roast

2 lb. middle cut of cod, 8 oz. onions, 1 oz
fat or dripping, 1 level teaspoon salt,
pinch of pepper.   Tomatoes can be used
instead of onions.

Remove any fins and make about four
shallow slashes across the back of the fish.
Cut one of the onions into thick slices and
place one of these in each slash. Dot the fish
with fat or dripping, sprinkle with salt and
pepper and put into a baking tin. Put the rest
of the onions round the fish and bake in a hot
oven for about half an hour until the fish is
cooked. Baste once or twice during cooking

other main meals with fish

OVEN FRIED FISH
1 level tablespoon flour, ½ level teaspoon
salt, pinch of pepper, pinch of grated nutmeg, 2 tablespoons milk, 1-1½ lb fillet of
fish, cut in pieces, browned breadcrumbs.

Blend flour, salt, pepper and nutmeg with
the milk. Dip the pieces of fish in this
and then roll in browned crumbs.
Arrange the fish in a well-greased pie-
dish and cover with greased paper Bake
in a hot oven for ½ hour. Note.—The
fish can be sprinkled with salt and pepper
and coated in breadcrumbs only.   If it
can be spared, up to 1 oz. cooking fat or
dripping can be heated in the pie-dish
before adding the fish.

BAKED STUFFED FISH
2 small haddock or whiting (about 1 lb each)
6 oz. stale bread or crusts, soaked and squeezed,
2 level tablespoons chopped parsley, 1 level teaspoon mixed dried herbs, 1 level tablespoon finely chopped onion, 2 level teaspoons salt, ¼ level
teaspoon pepper, 1 level tablespoon browned
breadcrumbs, ½ oz. dripping or cooking fat

Clean fish, leave head and tail on. Beat bread
with fork until smooth, add to parsley, herbs,
onion and seasoning.   Stuff fish with some of
mixture; sew up with needle and coarse cotton;
skewer into letter S form.   Place in a baking
tin, sprinkle with crumbs, dot with dripping.
Arrange remainder of stuffing in balls round
fish. Bake in moderate oven 15-20 minutes.
Remove skewers and thread.

Where there's Fish there's a Good Meal

fashion......

FASHION EDITOR : ROSEMARY CHUBB

Some of the best beachwear can be made at home from a yard or two of gaudy-bright cotton (salvaged, maybe, from last summer's too-short dress, or an old printed housecoat). It is made in the easiest way, from squares, triangles, or straight strips, gathered on to elastic, knotted, or darted here and there, and therefore easily adjustable for size. Observe the basic simplicity of the designs on these pages, which we have created for you to run up, from our instructions, in an hour or so: the closely knotted sarong-pantie and sun top in which you may swim without dismay: the tiny bloomers topped with a pie-frill bra—we like it bare-shouldered for an even tan, but you can attach shoulder straps for added safety if you wish: the artless triangular shawl and ballooning ruffled skirt—in these you may leave the beach with perfect propriety to take your lunch: and finally, the brief circular skirt, worn over minute pants, with a really firm, well-fitting brassière (recommended as an alternative to any of the other tops if you need something with a little more " support "). We suggest you make up these designs in imperial colours and dotted or exotically flowered prints. You need to be bold and brilliant to pay the sun the handsome compliment it deserves.

BRILLIANT BEACHWEAR

for you to make

Easily made sarong-pantie and bra.
From Bulletin No. A.6,
obtainable from Good Housekeeping
Needlework Department,
30 Grosvenor Gardens, S.W.1, price 6d.,
inclusive of postage to U.K. readers only.

Ruffled brassière, small pantie, scarf and skirt.
Instructions in Bulletin No. A.7,
obtainable from Good Housekeeping
Needlework Department,
30 Grosvenor Gardens, S.W.1,
price 9d., inclusive of postage to U.K. readers only.

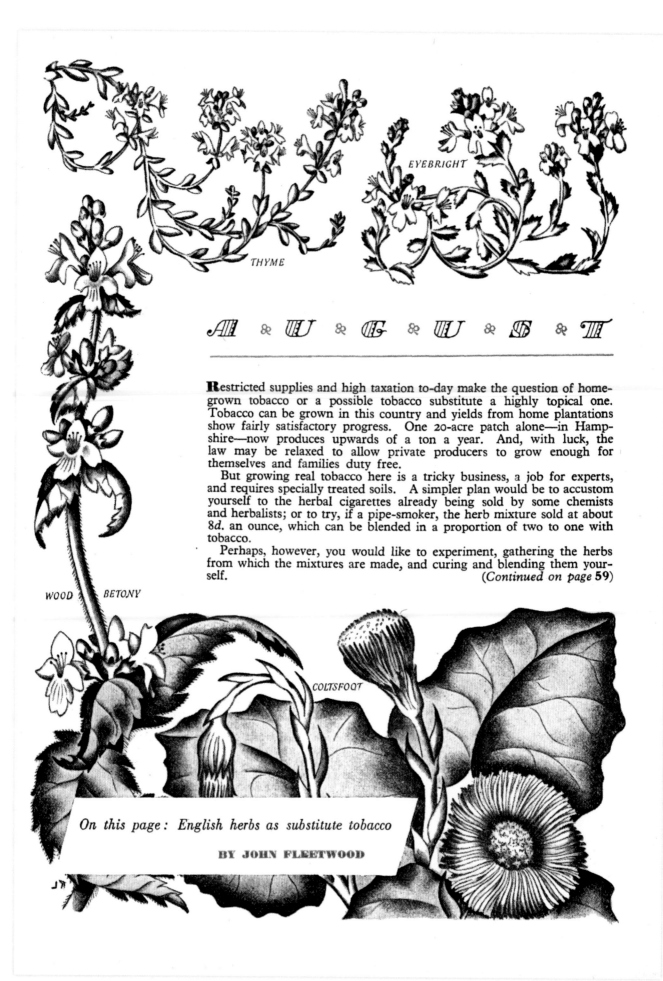

A ❦ U ❦ G ❦ U ❦ S ❦ T

Restricted supplies and high taxation to-day make the question of home-grown tobacco or a possible tobacco substitute a highly topical one. Tobacco can be grown in this country and yields from home plantations show fairly satisfactory progress. One 20-acre patch alone—in Hampshire—now produces upwards of a ton a year. And, with luck, the law may be relaxed to allow private producers to grow enough for themselves and families duty free.

But growing real tobacco here is a tricky business, a job for experts, and requires specially treated soils. A simpler plan would be to accustom yourself to the herbal cigarettes already being sold by some chemists and herbalists; or to try, if a pipe-smoker, the herb mixture sold at about 8d. an ounce, which can be blended in a proportion of two to one with tobacco.

Perhaps, however, you would like to experiment, gathering the herbs from which the mixtures are made, and curing and blending them yourself. *(Continued on page 59)*

EYEBRIGHT

THYME

WOOD BETONY

COLTSFOOT

On this page : English herbs as substitute tobacco

BY JOHN FLEETWOOD

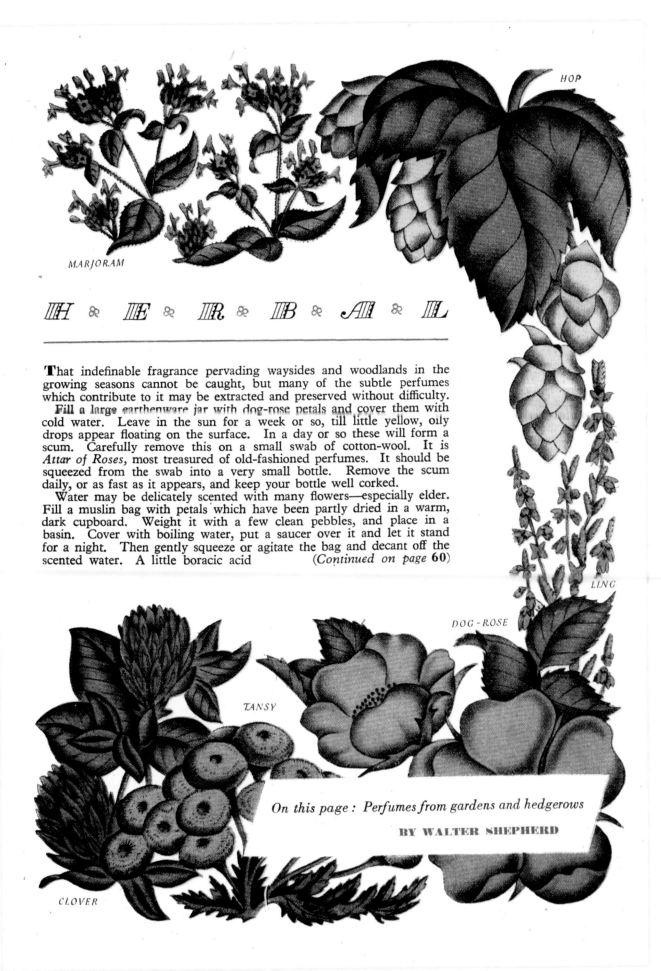

H & E & R & B & A & L

That indefinable fragrance pervading waysides and woodlands in the growing seasons cannot be caught, but many of the subtle perfumes which contribute to it may be extracted and preserved without difficulty.

Fill a large earthenware jar with dog-rose petals and cover them with cold water. Leave in the sun for a week or so, till little yellow, oily drops appear floating on the surface. In a day or so these will form a scum. Carefully remove this on a small swab of cotton-wool. It is *Attar of Roses,* most treasured of old-fashioned perfumes. It should be squeezed from the swab into a very small bottle. Remove the scum daily, or as fast as it appears, and keep your bottle well corked.

Water may be delicately scented with many flowers—especially elder. Fill a muslin bag with petals which have been partly dried in a warm, dark cupboard. Weight it with a few clean pebbles, and place in a basin. Cover with boiling water, put a saucer over it and let it stand for a night. Then gently squeeze or agitate the bag and decant off the scented water. A little boracic acid *(Continued on page* 60)

On this page : Perfumes from gardens and hedgerows

BY WALTER SHEPHERD

MARJORAM

HOP

LING

DOG-ROSE

TANSY

CLOVER

Television test—a first-class reception

Nat Allen and Orchestra are televised

These photographs take you, not into the busy television broadcasting studios at Alexandra Palace, but into the homes of those who " look in." They show actual images received on television screens and indicate how clear those receptions can be—a friendly smile from the commentator, a dance band in action, or a demonstrator showing how good jam should be made.

Leslie Mitchell as the viewer sees him

The performer is seen as well as heard

Joan Robins shows how to make good jam

Mr. Norman Collins, Controller of Television, with his wife and daughters

Photo : Fayer

Television spreads its wings

Here's a report on past progress, a forecast of developments to come, and a vivid sketch of the dynamic personality at the top

BY MARY BENEDETTA

Television, up to the present time, has been, in this country, a limited form of entertainment available only to those who live within transmission radius of Alexandra Palace, centre of the B.B.C. Television Service. This area extends roughly from the South Midlands to the South Coast, though enthusiasts outside this radius frequently send in reports of the clear receptions they have obtained, and, by a happy freak, a London transmission was, on one occasion, even received satisfactorily in the United States.

The opening of the first regional television transmitting station, at Sutton Coldfield, near Birmingham, which, it is hoped, will start to function some time next year, will bring television within reach of a much larger number of viewers; and will be followed by experiments to determine how many additional regional transmitting stations will ultimately be needed to make clear television reception possible in every part of the British Isles.

Alexandra Palace, however, will still remain the nerve centre of television in this country, for from there will be sent out all the programmes picked up by the (Continued on page 70)

A TEA COSY

in an 18th-century design

The Royal School of Needlework has adapted the wayward flowers on an 18th-century satin waistcoat to decorate a modern tea-cosy. Here we show half of the design ; it measures 13½ inches at the base, is 9 inches high. Transfer No. 1073 (for one side of tea-cosy only) and instructions cost 8d., from Good Housekeeping Needlework Department, 30 Grosvenor Gardens. We are happy to announce that limited quantities of " Sheba " and " Clark's Stranded Cotton " are also available from that address for working the design. Skeins for one side of cosy, in the colours shown here, with transfer and instructions, cost 4s. 3d.

GOOD HOUSEKEEPING'S COOKERY BOOK

CUTS OF MUTTON OR LAMB AND HOW TO TREAT THEM

Scrag end of neck	..	Stew or braise.
Middle neck	..	braise.
Best end of neck—in the piece	..	Roast or braise.
Best end of neck—when cut into cutlets	..	Fry or grill.
Loin—in the piece	..	Roast.
Loin—when cut into chops	..	Fry or grill.
Leg	..	or boil.
Shoulder	..	Roast—can be bo and stuffed if liked.
Breast	..	Stew.
Breast—if bone	..	Can be stuffed roasted, or braised.
Sheep's head	..	Stew and broth.
Trotters	..	Stew.

CONTENTS INCLUDE

Nearly 2,000 recipes

Meal planning

Shopping and Storing

Utensils and Appliances

Economical Cookery

Preserving

Wines

Invalid Cookery

32 pages of photographs

12 colour plates

BOILED LEG OF MUTTON AND CAPER SAUCE

½ leg of mutton	4 carrots, turnips and onions of
Boiling water	medium size
Salt and pepper	Caper sauce (page 29s)

Wipe the meat. Have ready sufficient fast-boiling water to cover completely the joint to be cooked. Place the joint in this, and when the w again reaches boiling point, allow it to boil for a few minutes. Then sufficient salt and pepper to flavour, and the vegetables cut into quart Allow to simmer ... rmal time to al is 20 minutes to the lb. and 20 minutes over. When cooking is aln complete, prepare the caper sauce, using the liquid from the pot. S the meat on a hot dish, put the vegetables round and pour over the ca sauce.

Neck of mutton may be treated in the same way.

BRAISED LAMB CUTLETS AND GREEN PEAS

1 on	1 lump sugar
4 lamb cutlets	A little water
2–3 young turnips	1 cupful green peas
Seasoning	Chopped parsley

e oni ... an earthenware casser im the cutlets and lay them on the top. Add the turnips, seasoning and sugar. Pour in water, nearly covering the put the lid on, and stew very gently for ½ hour. Then add the p freshly shelled, ... hot a little finely-chopped parsley sprinkled over the top.

Note: Mutton cutlets or a piece of fillet of veal could be cooked in same way, allowing rather longer time. The cooking may be done eit in the oven or on ... The ... able may be varied, and yo carrots, tomato, French beans, shredded celery, etc., used instead of gr peas.

Good Housekeeping's Cookery Book: 928 pages, demy octavo in cloth boards, 42s.

an all-inclusive guide to modern cookery

At last *Good Housekeeping's Cookery Book* is ready. Between its washable white covers, clad in a colourful dust-jacket, there are nearly 2,000 tested recipes, and a vast amount of other useful information.

When compiling this book, our aim was to provide a complete work of reference for future generations of cooks, but at the same time to meet the needs of present-day austerity. With this in view, many dishes have alternative recipes, one using plain and the other richer ingredients.

Although it begins with the simplest basic processes, the Cookery Book is by no means for beginners only. In fact, we believe it will prove to be a classic in the realm of cookery literature. It contains sections on meal planning, shopping and storing, cooking equipment, and so on, as well as recipes for every type of dish.

Good Housekeeping's Cookery Book can be obtained from any good bookseller, or from Good Housekeeping Shopping Centre, 30 Grosvenor Gdns., S.W.1, price 42s., or 43s. by post.

A plan for

CHRISTMAS CATERING

*with Greetings from
the Institute*

In the following pages we have kept to the old traditional dishes, only simplifying these here and there in accord with present-day limitations, for we know that at Christmas-time the old ways always seem the best ways. Although we realise only too well that it is difficult for the housewife to have a restful holiday, we are convinced that much can be done by planning in advance and getting the cooking well forward to ensure that you are not too tired to enjoy the festivities with the rest of the family.

If you are expecting extra guests over the holiday, look out and wash ready for use the extra plates, glasses and cutlery which you will require, not forgetting the large dish for the Christmas bird. Decide on your table decorations, being certain that the linen you wish to use is freshly laundered.

In the kitchen, check up on the ingredients required for your cookery. Make a list of things you need to purchase and get them in good time, leaving only perishable things until the last minute.

Take your pudding from the store cupboard on Christmas Eve ready to heat up on Christmas morning, and prepare and stuff the bird.

A very Happy Christmas to you all! We shall think of you as we sit down to our own dinners and visualise the many perfectly cooked turkeys throughout the land which we hope the following pages may help to achieve.

GOOD HOUSEKEEPING INSTITUTE PRINCIPAL: PHYLLIS L. GARBUTT

Ice-cream is always a first favourite, especially when lavishly adorned with fruit

W ho's

BY GERTRUDE TULLIS
(Combined Domestic Subjects Diploma, Gloucester)

There are few people who do not at times have an irresistible longing for something sweet, and sugar, dietitians tell us, gives us energy more quickly than any other food. However, the struggle between the desire for something sweet now and home-made jam later on need not be too bothersome. Here are half a dozen recipes which make use of jam, marmalade, syrup or honey for sweetening, and a special one with extra sugar.

MARMALADE WHIP

¾ oz. gelatine
3 to 4 dessertspoonfuls sweet orange marmalade
1 tin evaporated milk
1 orange and chocolate to decorate

Dissolve the gelatine in a little hot water. Add to the marmalade and milk. Whisk until thick and frothy. Pour into a large dessert dish or individual glasses. Decorate with orange slices and grated chocolate.

HONEY FRUIT BOATS

4 oz. shortcrust pastry
2 oz. honey
2 oz. breadcrumbs
2 oz. raisins, sultanas, etc.

Grated rind of 1 orange or lemon
Orange or lemon juice
Glacé cherries for decorating

Roll the pastry thinly, and line boat-shaped or tartlet tins. Prick, and bake " blind " in a hot oven (450° F.) for 10-15 minutes. Mix the honey, breadcrumbs, dried fruit, fruit rind and sufficient juice to give a soft consistency. Fill the cases and decorate.

OATEN MERINGUE FLAN

6 oz. shortcrust pastry
8 oz. rolled oats
2 oz. glacé cherries or preserved ginger
6 tablespoonfuls warmed syrup
Juice of 1 lemon
1 egg
1 oz. margarine
Button meringues

Roll out the pastry and line a Swiss roll tin with it. Crimp the edges. Mix well the oats, glacé cherries or ginger, syrup, lemon juice, yolk of egg and melted fat. Spread the mixture over the pastry and decorate the top with pastry strips. Bake in a moderately hot oven (375° F.) for

about 35-40 minutes. Top the pie with button meringues made from the egg white, using the recipe given on page 37, and decorate with pieces of preserved ginger or glacé cherries. Serve cold or hot with a syrup sauce.

PEPPERMINT DESSERT

2 oz. peppermint rock
1 pint milk
1 tablespoonful rennet
Colouring (optional)
Nuts, glacé fruit or chocolate for decorating

Crush rock, dissolve in warmed milk which must not be allowed to become more than lukewarm. Stir in the rennet and the colouring. Put at once into individual glasses and leave to set. Decorate.

CHILDREN'S SUNDÆ

1 dessertspoonful cornflour
¾ pint sweetened condensed milk (diluted)
1 oz. margarine
Few drops vanilla essence
Banana, cherries or other fruit
Chocolate or jam sauce
Chopped nuts (optional)
Ice-cream wafers

Blend the cornflour with a little of the milk. Heat the rest and add the blended mixture. Boil for 2–3 minutes, stirring all the time. Remove from heat and add the margarine and vanilla. Turn into a bowl and whisk. When cool, pour into freezing trays and turn refrigerator to " coldest." When firm at edges, return to bowl and whisk again. Then return to frig. When frozen, scoop two spoonfuls into chilled glass dishes together with the mixed fruit. Top with chocolate or jam sauce and a few chopped nuts, if liked. Serve with wafers.

MARMALADE SLICES

½ lb. shortcrust pastry
Marmalade
Orange glacé icing
Orange jellies for decorating

Make the shortcrust pastry and roll it out to a rectangular shape. Spread thickly with marmalade and put another piece of pastry over the top. Seal the edges, and mark into slices. Bake in a hot oven (400° F.) for 15–20 minutes. Allow to cool and cut into fingers. Spread with orange or vanilla glacé icing and decorate.

HONEY FUDGE

1 lb. sugar
4 oz. honey
3 tablespoonfuls water
¼ teaspoonful cream of tartar
1 egg white
¼ teaspoonful vanilla essence

Put the sugar, honey, water and cream of tartar into a strong pan, bring slowly to boiling point and boil gently until it reaches a temperature of 280° F. Whisk the egg white and pour the hot syrup into this slowly. Beat vigorously. Add the essence and, when thick, pour into a greased tin. When cold, cut into squares with a greased knife.

HONEY BALLS

Chop equal quantities of peal and dates and a few glacé cherries. Add enough warmed honey to make them stick together. Divide into small equal-sized portions and roll in chopped nuts or a mixture of cocoa and icing-sugar. Stand to harden and serve in paper cases.

got a sweet tooth?

If that's your weakness, here are ways of giving yourself a treat

Tiny meringues and glacé cherries make a colourful decoration for this flan

the institute

PRINCIPAL: PHYLLIS L. GARBUTT

When leafy beech trees throw cool shadows on the shorn, sweet-smelling lawn, and full-blown roses drop their petals one by one on the dry earth, then is the time to entertain in the garden. There is a leisurely, leave-your-cares-behind atmosphere about having a few friends to tea, or even about garden parties on a larger scale. Whether the excuse for the party is tennis or cricket, or to collect funds for the restoration of the village clock-tower, the food must be simple, and not too elaborately served.

Sooner or later, the somnolent bumbling of the bees at their nectar-bars will drive even the most active guests in search of shade and food. The use of garden tables or light ones brought out for the occasion, of gay coloured cloths or formal white, is a matter of personal choice. The important point is to choose a shady position, as no food and few guests really like the full heat of the sun.

Bring the food out just when it is required. Anticipate the heavy demands that will be made on drinks and prepare plenty of fruit drinks, tea, hot or iced, or iced coffee.

Photo by Casparius. Plates by Branksome Ceramics Ltd. Glassware and tray by Peter Jones

Christmas Fare

Here are recipes for popular Christmas items. You'll find that, though they're not extravagant with ingredients, they give you the traditional Christmassy flavour.

THE CHRISTMAS ROAST

Suitable joints are ribs of beef, breast of lamb or veal, loin of lamb or veal. Approximate size for 4 people will be 3 lb. Joints should be boned before stuffing, and surplus fat removed.
STUFFING : 6 oz. breadcrumbs, 2 tablespoons chopped parsley, 1 level teaspoon mixed herbs, 1 level teaspoon dried egg, dry, 2 level teaspoons salt, ½ level teaspoon pepper, 1 ½ oz. dripping, lard or chopped suet,

2 tablespoons milk, stock or water. Mix together the breadcrumbs, parsley, herbs, dried egg and seasonings. Melt the fat in the milk, stock or water, and add to the dry ingredients. Mix well with a fork and spread a layer of mixture along the inside of the meat. Roll meat up into a neat shape and tie with string or tape to keep it in shape. Bake in a hot oven for 10 minutes, reduce heat to slow or moderate and continue cooking for a further 1 ¼-1 ½ hours. Make any remaining stuffing into balls, fry or bake them separately and serve round the meat.

MAKING THE CAKE

3 oz. sugar, 4 oz. margarine, 3 level tablespoons warmed treacle or syrup, 8 oz. plain flour, ½ level teaspoon bicarbonate of soda, pinch of salt, 1 level teaspoon cinnamon, 1 level teaspoon mixed spice, 2 eggs, fresh or dried, 1 lb. mixed dried fruit, 3 tablespoons cold tea.
Cream the sugar and margarine together and beat in the treacle or syrup. Mix the flour, soda, salt and spices together. Add alternately with the eggs to the creamed mixture and beat well. Add the fruit and mix in the tea. Put the mixture into a 7 in. tin, lined with greased paper,

and bake in a very moderate oven for 2½ hours.
ICING : 6 oz. icing sugar, 1 tablespoon water, few drops lemon juice or lemon substitute.
Sift sugar into a bowl to remove lumps, add water and lemon juice and mix till smooth with a wooden spoon. Spread with knife on cake, dipping knife into water occasionally to give a smooth surface. This is sufficient for a thin layer on top of 7 in. cake.

A DELICIOUS MINCEMEAT

½-¾ lb. mixed dried fruit, 4 oz. apples, 3-4 oz. sugar, 2-4 oz. suet or melted margarine, 2 level tablespoons marmalade, ½ level teaspoon mixed spice, ½ level teaspoon cinnamon, 1 level teaspoon grated nutmeg, ¼ level teaspoon salt, ½ level teaspoon of lemon juice or lemon essence,

and a few drops of rum essence if you like. Chop the dried fruit finely and grate apples. Add other ingredients and mix very thoroughly. Put into small jars and tie down securely. Store in a cool dry place. If the larger quantities of fruit, sugar and fat are used, this will keep for several weeks, but with the smaller amounts, it should be used within about 10 days. (CII)

ISSUED BY THE MINISTRY OF FOOD